3.50

Athlone French P...

Athlone French Poets

General editor EILEEN LE BRETON

Reader in French Language and Literature,
Bedford College University of London

MONOGRAPHS

Verlaine *by C. Chadwick*

Gérard de Nerval *by Norma Rinsler*

Saint-John Perse *by Roger Little*

CRITICAL EDITIONS

Paul Valéry: Charmes ou Poèmes
edited by Charles G. Whiting

Paul Verlaine: Sagesse
edited by C. Chadwick

Gérard de Nerval: Les Chimères
edited by Norma Rinsler

Saint-John Perse: Exil
edited by Roger Little

SAINT-JOHN PERSE

Exil

edited by
ROGER LITTLE

UNIVERSITY OF LONDON
THE ATHLONE PRESS
1973

Published by
THE ATHLONE PRESS
UNIVERSITY OF LONDON
at 4 Gower Street, London WC1

Distributed by
Tiptree Book Services Ltd
Tiptree, Essex

U.S.A. and Canada
Humanities Press Inc
New York

0 485 14706 8 *cloth*
0 485 12706 7 *paperback*

Printed in Great Britain by
The Garden City Press Limited
Letchworth, Hertfordshire
SG6 1JS

Athlone French Poets

General Editor EILEEN LE BRETON

This series is designed to provide students and general readers both with Monographs on important nineteenth-and twentieth-century French poets and Critical Editions of representative works by these poets.

The Monographs aim at presenting the essential biographical facts while placing the poet in his social and intellectual context. They contain a detailed analysis of his poetical works and, where appropriate, a brief account of his other writings. His literary reputation is examined and his contribution to the development of French poetry is assessed, as is also his impact on other literatures. A selection of critical views and a bibliography are appended.

The Critical Editions contain a substantial introduction aimed at presenting each work against its historical background as well as studying its genre, structure, themes, style, etc. and highlighting its relevance for today. The text normally given is the complete text of the original edition. It is followed by full commentaries on the poems and annotation of the text, including variant readings when these are of real significance, and a select bibliography.

E. Le B.

PREFACE

This is the first attempt at a closely annotated edition of the complete cycle of poems in Saint-John Perse's *Exil*. Its aim is not to impose a view of the poems—though inevitably my own will come through—but to guide the reader towards his own informed assessment and towards a further and perhaps closer reading of the text itself. Its manner is therefore informative rather than exclusive; my own high regard for the work, implicit, I trust, in my enthusiasm, does not exclude awareness of the criticisms of inscrutability and even 'flatulence' levelled at Perse's work.[1] Analytically, however, such attitudes are sterile, and I have purposely not sought to impose a synthesis.

The reason for omitting certain general considerations from this book is partly practical: it is published simultaneously with a companion volume, *Saint-John Perse*, referred to here simply as 'the monograph', which serves as an introduction to the life of Alexis Leger and to the poetry of Saint-John Perse. The two volumes are meant to be read in conjunction, and the present edition of *Exil* is conceived as a satellite to the planet monograph, each making complete sense only in relation to the other, though with the planet evidently having the edge in an imagined independent existence.

Because this is an annotated rather than a critical edition, textual variants have not been indicated. In fact there are none of major significance, and the few there are generally arise from the precarious circumstances of wartime publication in various countries rather than from a change of mind on Perse's part. I have therefore used the text revised and corrected by Saint-John Perse for the 1960 edition of his *Œuvre poétique*, reprinted in the Bibliothèque de la Pléiade (Gallimard, 1972), and concentrated on elucidating meanings, indicating comparisons and presenting interpretations. In doing so I am indebted to earlier critical work on the poems: when quoting another critic I am tacitly acknowledging my gratitude, even where there is an area of disagreement, since he has doubtless helped me towards a clearer formulation of my own position. Constantly in the back of my mind has lurked Perse's memorable phrase: 'Un livre, c'est la mort d'un arbre.' As I wrote my introduction to this volume in my study, often staring blankly out at the pear-tree left as a mutilated stump by the builders, the image imprinted itself on my mind with particular power. Criticism certainly cannot replace Perse's admirable poems, and it should aim never to distract the reader from the text, for that is the living tree grown to maturity and perpetuated by the poet's generosity.

R.L.

CONTENTS

ACKNOWLEDGEMENT

The cover portrait of Saint-John Perse was made by Baron Scotford of the Silhouette Studios, London, in 1912. It was kindly lent by the poet for the present series and the author, general editor and publisher wish to thank him for permission to reproduce it for the first time.

To Sam and Louis, with gratitude and affection

INTRODUCTION

When 'Exil' was published in 1942, it broke Saint-John Perse's poetic silence which had lasted since the appearance of *Anabase* in 1924. In the meantime, Alexis Leger, the diplomat behind the pen-name Saint-John Perse, had risen from being a 'secrétaire d'ambassade' at the Quai d'Orsay to being its permanent general secretary with the rank and title of ambassador. In 1940 he was removed from office and went into exile in the United States. The four poems that constitute the *Exil* tetralogy, namely 'Exil', 'Pluies' (published in 1943), 'Neiges' (1944) and 'Poème à l'Etrangère' (1943) represent one man's reaction to the tragic circumstances in which war had placed him. But they are neither private lamentations nor circumstantial verses: they explore the nature of exile as a constant not only of man's political state, or statelessness, but, more particularly, of his spiritual condition, of his exile in relation to the unknown and unknowable mystery of life. When the scientist is asking 'how?' or even 'what?', the poet must in addition still dare to ask 'why?', and his intuition as well as his example will guide the scientist and other men.

By their aspirations, therefore, as well as by the original nature of Perse's writing, these poems are, in a referential sense, impervious to the traditional methods of *explication de texte*. They are inventive entities and only disruption of their dynamic flow can follow from our hanging on a particular word or phrase to explain in prose the multiple poetic effects at work, the more so as our prosaic investigations are doomed to be half-truths. This is especially true where reference is made in the notes to other writers: the little letters 'cf.' bear a heavy responsibility. In the notes to this volume, they do not imply: 'Saint-John Perse has read this book and remembered this phrase' but: 'You may care to consider the similarity, affinity or contrast between the two texts'. Consequently such comparisons must be taken to indicate the gratuitous limitations of the critic's reading rather than any 'source' of Perse's poetry. For the source lies elsewhere: not in books but in the creative imagination transmuting real experiences and real perceptions into the *vraisemblance* of the poem, 'la réalité poétique, plus que la vérité scientifique . . . étant en raison inverse de l'exactitude littérale' (Pléiade, p. 561).[2] One must never forget that in consulting a work of this nature, with its inevitable concentration, particularly in the notes, on the *letter* of the poetry, there is a constant danger of overlooking the far more essential *spirit* of the poetry.

That spirit is less involved with immediate political circumstances than with a broader view of man tragically aware of the limitations and ambivalence of his condition. Yet the reasons for the sense of grief against which Perse makes his very positive and optimistic stand were profoundly real. He wrote of 'toute la crainte que j'éprouve parfois de laisser apparaître ma tristesse' (Pléiade, p. 898) and refers to his 'armure d'exilé' as 'l'habit du scaphandrier' (p. 901); it is a proud kind of humility. The imposition of limits seemed to make him even more aware of the vital necessity of discovering where human limits lie—physically, intellectually, linguistically and spiritually—and of striving to probe beyond them.

The Political Background

The four poems of *Exil* are not Resistance poems but poems of exile. Once that is said and its implications understood, any detailed analysis of the reasons for Leger's removal from office in May 1940 is clearly irrelevant: the fact itself is sufficient to have stimulated in Perse's mind the poems reprinted here. As head of the Quai d'Orsay since February 1933, after a meteoric rise to the top of his chosen profession, he had served under successive governments of different persuasions with an honorable consistency of purpose, opposing appeasement with Nazi Germany as tenaciously as he upheld the ideals of international cooperation with all countries prepared both to be free and to respect the freedom of others.

Truth and objectivity are war's first casualties. Historians are still engaged, as they will be for years to come, in unravelling the tangle of plot and accusation, still sufficiently recent to rouse fierce partisan passions, which surrounds the events of May and

June 1940 when Hitler's implacable Panzer divisions took advantage of French divisiveness. Defence arrangements which had proved their worth in bygone days—the horse being preferred to the tank, the messenger to the radio-telephone, the Maginot line to the aeroplane—were applied regardless of technical developments offering increased manœuvrability. The story would be comic if it were not so tragic. Against this background, Leger's fate was sealed by 'les intrigues personnelles d'une camarilla privée qui ont réussi à abuser Paul Reynaud'.[3] The leaders of the attack were Paul Baudouin and Reynaud's scheming and power-hungry mistress, the Comtesse Hélène de Portes. These defeatists enjoyed the active or moral support of all those intent on making peace at any price as well as of Leger's political enemies, who were essentially those who had been Aristide Briand's opponents before his death in 1932. Leger thus found himself the politicians' scapegoat, the one man who despite his position of authority could not, as a civil servant, dictate terms to the ministers whose wishes it was his function to serve. His situation was by its nature precarious, and one admires his attempts to bring continuity of action to international relationships which are not only shifting by definition but which were specifically altered by the very varied attitudes of the numerous foreign ministers under whom he served. One has only to think of the succession of premiers during the pre-war years: Herriot, a radical-socialist, was followed by four others only one of whom stayed in office for more than three months. After Laval who inaugurated the policy of appeasement, Léon Blum headed the Front populaire, and so it continued. Reynaud's own cabinet which took over in March 1940 included a hotch-potch of socialists, radical-socialists, and left-of-centre moderates, with a conservative at its head disliked by the right wing. Dissension alone could be the outcome, and it is scarcely surprising to find intrigue rife and petty bickering distracting attention from the imminent catastrophe.

The experience Leger had gained both 'in the field' in the early years of his career and at the Quai d'Orsay since 1922 as well as his firmness of purpose and moral courage gave his advice particular authority, but the politicians were free to follow or flout it. He was reported in 1936 as saying: 'Notre premier devoir est une absolue loyauté, et l'on n'a aucune peine à le faire comprendre à des hommes d'honneur: c'est un principe qui ne souffre auncune restriction mentale, non seulement à l'égard du Ministre, cela va de soi, mais à l'égard du régime' (Pléiade, pp. 598–9). It is not difficult to see why such a man could not remain in office when Reynaud had broken the code of honour essential for the trust between a Foreign Minister and the principal executive of his ideas. For Reynaud proved too weak to withstand the pressure brought by Baudouin and his mistress. Exhausted by his functions as both prime and foreign minister, he determined simultaneously to replace Leger by a yes-man and to hand over the Foreign Ministry to Daladier (to be replaced subsequently by Baudouin himself) who would therefore be left to do the explaining. The sop to be offered Leger was the post of ambassador in Washington with the specific and urgent mission of bringing the United States into the war. The plan was settled between Baudouin and Reynaud on the evening of 18 May. Daladier was summoned and asked to inform Leger of the decision to send him to Washington on a mission so delicate that he alone could accomplish it. Leger was duly told the same night, but rejected the idea as absurd at that stage and, sensing the intrigue, declared that if he were to be removed from office he would accept none other. Only the following morning did he learn that he was no longer Secrétaire Général, when one of his secretaries showed him the announcement in the *Journal officiel*. He alone had the courage to demand his diplomatic 'mise en disponibilité', declaring as he handed the official request over: 'J'ai droit à toute l'injustice' (*Honneur*, p. 768).

A letter written to President Herriot a few days later from Arcachon, where Leger had gone to join his mother, presents with admirable restraint the circumstances of his dismissal (Pléiade, pp. 601–3). Gnawed by the worm of defeatism in his cabinet, Reynaud was soon to succumb himself and be replaced by the collaborationist conjunction of Laval, Weygand and Pétain. By mid-June the Germans had marched triumphant into Paris. On 22 June, the armistice was signed: the war in France was over.

Throughout his period of office, Leger had been untiring in his efforts to maintain and improve good relations between France, Britain and the U.S.A. The policies of international cooperation which he had patiently pursued were based on the firm belief that these three countries had essentially common interests and a similar view of honour and democracy. The faction bent on appeasement with the Nazis would obviously stop at nothing to eliminate such a man, and Berlin was understandably delighted at his removal. The director of *Le Petit Parisien* declared:

Je ne crois pas qu'il y ait pareil exemple de manque d'égards envers un fonctionnaire contre qui on ne pouvait relever aucune faute professionnelle. Mais l'escamotage auquel on avait dû recourir et la lâcheté avec laquelle il était accompli, puisque personne n'avait osé en prendre la responsabilité, dépassaient la personnalité de M. Leger, si éminente qu'elle soit; les vrais responsables . . . ouvraient délibérément la première brèche dans l'alliance franco-britannique. (*Honneur*, p. 767)

It was natural then that Leger, when obliged to leave his own country which was scarcely recognisable as such, should choose to spend his exile in Britain and the United States.

On 16 June he embarked on a cargo vessel bound for England. While a number of his literary friends were singing Pétain's praises or accepting dictatorship as the only alternative to national decomposition,[4] Leger was steadfast, and more subtle, in his opposition to either extreme. Being totally behind the idea of Resistance groups abroad and irreducibly opposed to Pétain's armistice government, he supported de Gaulle's Free French movement in every respect but one, and that was in the claim it made to be the official French government. 'Un tel "gouvernement", dénué de tout mandat légal, n'eût pu même, moralement, invoquer une légitimation de fait, l'assentiment national français ne pouvant alors s'exprimer' (Pléiade, p. 633). The fact that 'la France libre' was supported financially by a foreign government made the notion of a self-appointed French national government even less acceptable. Leger therefore stayed as a private citizen with his opposite number, Lord Vansittart, at Denham House in Buckinghamshire for three weeks. He left England at the same time as the country's bullion reserves on the Monarch of Bermuda, bound for Canada. The motivation for his departure is explained clearly in a letter to a German historian:

mon départ d'Angleterre ne tendait nullement à me 'désolidariser des réfugiés francais', mais, bien au contraire, à rechercher en Amérique l'élargissement de la solidarité étrangère en faveur de la France libre et résistante, dans un élargissement du cadre d'action interalliée. (Pléiade, p. 633)

On Bastille Day 1940, Leger arrived in New York. His Paris flat had been ransacked by the Gestapo when the Germans took the capital, and he was soon to learn that all his possessions were further sequestered on the orders of the Vichy government, in this as in so many other ways outdoing the Nazis in their prosecution of fascist orders. Late in October a decree was issued to deprive him of French nationality, restored to him only after the Liberation. Although without a source of income, he refused tempting offers to publish his memoirs and moved to Washington to take up a post as literary adviser to the Library of Congress. Payment came not from the government, something Leger would not have accepted, but from a special fund donated by private citizens and administered by the Librarian, Archibald MacLeish. He continued to give active support to the cause of the Resistance as well as to share his unrivalled knowledge of the French situation and its sources with his friends among the leaders of his host nation. Churchill was not alone in adding his voice to de Gaulle's to plead with Leger to join forces with 'la France libre' in London, but the reply was always the same, polite but firm:

Diplomate de métier, n'entendant assumer que la direction d'une action diplomatique, je ne saurais m'associer à l'activité directrice du Comité de Londres sans accentuer encore, en apparence comme en réalité, le caractère politique qu'on lui reproche. Ce serait inopportun pour le mouvement de la 'France libre'; ce serait contraire à la conception que je me fais moi-même de son rôle. (Pléiade, p. 614)

All his faith in a policy to bring unity to Europe, to reinforce the Anglo-French partnership, to contain Nazi Germany, which he had, in complete accord with Briand, pursued unstintingly before the war shied at the stumbling-block of what he perhaps rather legalistically saw as de Gaulle's undemocratic and unconstitutional claim to head a government. His contempt was reserved for the collaborators, the right wing that had violently opposed treating with Hitler in time and had now found acceptable 'l'offre de collaboration faite, sur pied de guerre, au profit d'un ordre germanique, par une Allemagne totalitaire, impérialiste et raciste à une France asservie, opprimée et isolée . . .' (Pléiade, p. 611).

Such integrity, such steadfastness of purpose is perhaps one side of a coin of which the other is inflexibility. It has been suggested that 'there was something unyielding in the pattern of his diplomacy',[5] but it was not *his* diplomacy that was in question or at fault. He was a civil servant carrying out the decisions of his ministers: it was they who bore the responsibilities of government. If Leger's own views coincided fully with those of some of them—Briand, Barthou, Herriot for example—no such thing could be said of his necessary collaboration with others, such as Laval. Twice he submitted his resignation as secrétaire général; twice it was refused. Successive ministers made use of him in different ways, and if French policies failed in the chaotic blindness that led to France's defeat, a mere executive should not be made the scapegoat. In moral, and therefore in diplomatic terms, one cannot but wonder at Leger's integrity and consistency. For if his lofty conception of France's role—*gesta Dei per Francos*—to create harmony among peoples belongs to a less violent age, it bears all the more witness to his value as a restraining influence on the shifting and often shifty policies of French Foreign Ministers after Briand. Indeed his vision of a united Europe seems at last to be partially realised. For he had 'l'attribut essentiel de l'homme d'Etat et du diplomate: le sens des possibilités' (Pléiade, p. 609). It was his sense of the possible, within the strict code of honour by which he lived, that allowed him to overcome the material and, more importantly, the spiritual deprivation of exile by turning to poetry.

The Poems

THE CIRCUMSTANCES OF THEIR COMPOSITION

Someone so deeply involved in the tragic events of 1940 as Leger was, someone whose personal suffering was so thoroughly enmeshed in the general agony could not escape unmoved or unscathed. The echoes of his exile reverberate through the poems of *Exil*, all written before the end of the war in Europe. Perse's poetry is so far from abstraction that however much it aims at, and succeeds in attaining to the intemporal and universal, it remains firmly rooted in the concrete and the real. His statement that '*Exil* n'est pas une image de la Résistance' (Pléiade, p. 576) needs therefore to be seen as a riposte to those critics who had wished to see in his work *nothing but* references to immediate circumstances. Seeing the declaration in this light, as a refusal to accept the limitations imposed by partial critics (and the first book to appear in French on Perse, by Saillet, performed a notable disservice in this respect), one is free to appreciate that elements from the poet's personal life and from the world situation have their contribution to make in a full understanding of the poems. As we shall see, each poem in the tetralogy depends for the inspiration of its image-structure on the particular chance of immediate circumstances and yet far transcends them, expressing not only the pain of exile as a geographical removal from one's homeland but also the sense of exile as an integral part of man's spiritual nature.

'Exil': *written Long Beach Island, New Jersey, 1941; first published Chicago, 1942*

After Leger had worked for a few months in the Library of Congress, he was invited by Francis Biddle, then Attorney-General of the U.S.A., and his wife Katherine, to spend some ten days with them in June 1941 at their beach-house on Long Beach Island, New Jersey. It was there, on the high dunes not far from the red-brick Barnegat lighthouse, that 'Exil' was written. Perse does not shy from referring directly to the beach, the lighthouse or his hosts and their holiday home (canto 1), nor in more oblique terms to the occupation of France and its effects on his fellow-countrymen. Yet on the relatively few occasions when there may be some echo of the war, other interpretations of the lines are much more important. Thus although the word 'exode' occurs, the word used for the flight of refugees from Paris and the northern part of France before the advancing German troops, the context (iii, 2) suggests rather some classical or biblical past. Similarly 'l'oiseau de Barbarie' (vii, 6) has been interpreted as the emblem of the barbarian invasion, the Prussian eagle, and seems to make good sense as such, particularly as Perse is normally attracted to birds and their song but here insists: 'Exècre, ô femme, sous ton toit un chant d'oiseau de Barbarie . . .' Yet even if Germans were billeted with the lady in question, it is difficult to claim more than considerable indirectness for the reference. The poet's separation from his loved ones is far more important in the context, and while a particular phrase may leave us puzzling there is no doubt about the emotion generated. For here, and throughout the poem, despite the complexities, the theme and texture of the writing are firmly held around the single, though many-sided, idea of exile and the central image chosen as its objective correlative, the beach. This is a powerful force for both coherence and sympathy when, through all its extensions and associations, it is known to be a particular beach such as anyone may be acquainted with, a measure for the reader to gauge Perse's creative originality against the basic, familiar data.

Images of the sea have special significance because it represents both the distance between France and the United States and the means of covering that distance. Perse declares: 'Me voici restitué à ma rive natale' (v, 3), and it is literally as well as metaphysically true. His first years, spent in Guadeloupe, had given him both a deep love and knowledge of the sea and also a sense that it was 'hantée d'invisibles départs' ('Pour fêter une enfance', v); now it is 'cette mer qui n'est jamais l'exil, étant tout l'exil', as Perse wrote to Katherine Biddle, recalling the words he had used on first sighting the sea on Long Beach Island.[6] Its presence in the poem is justified, in so far as it needs justification in Perse's poetics, by its littoral presence before the beach-house. It further admits the inclusion of images of fish and gulls, of coral and foam, and while playing one role in the spatial dialectic of the beach as a threshold plays another when it is itself considered as the threshold to France and to the secular eternity of which the sea, for the poet, is a symbol.

Nor need we doubt the reality of the thunder and lightning or the fierce June sun which have their important parts to play in the poem. Perse prefers to conserve his energy for invention for the process of structuring his poem rather than dissipate it on the trivial; he accepts and sifts the perceptions of his senses rather than attempting to distort the data. His keen powers of observation contributed to the tolerability of exile; a whole new world opened up before him and helped him to overcome his belief, expressed to MacLeish on settling in Washington, that he would never write poetry again. The insistent demands of poetic inspiration could not be silenced in the face of so many new experiences, so they had to be controlled by a process of selection and organisation. It was a process that, in the circumstances, demanded immense courage, but in 'Exil' we see Perse turning the tables on exile, creating from loss and deprivation the dynamic and positive force of the poem.

'Pluies': *written Savannah, Georgia, 1943; first published Buenos Aires, 1943*

Although 'Poème à l'Etrangère' was the next of the four poems to be written, convenience suggests our acceptance of the poet's chosen order. Reasons of structure largely determined that order, suggesting certain patterns of development which would otherwise have been more confused or even lost.[7]

'Pluies' is an inland poem, and continues the sense of immobility and of self-reliance as well as the essential dialogue between poetry and silence of 'Exil'. Charlton Ogburn has given, so to speak, an eye-witness account of its genesis (*Honneur*, pp. 273–9). The poet had been travelling around Georgia with friends in the late autumn of 1942. When they were in Savannah, a long drought came to a spectacular end one night: 'Peu après notre arrivée à l'hôtel, dans la soirée, la digue du ciel se rompit, et l'averse torrentielle, mêlée d'éclairs, fut parmi nous. Leger s'était levé, nous laissait. A la fenêtre de sa chambre, ouverte au Sud, il allait s'installer pour le reste de la nuit . . . Nous sûmes plus tard, en dépit de sa farouche discrétion en matière littéraire, qu'il s'était attablé à l'aube pour écrire. Il emportait dans son carnet de voyageur—ce carnet noir à feuilles détachables que nous l'avions vu parfois tirer furtivement de sa poche—le premier état du long poème: "Pluies" '. In the early editions it was dated 'Savannah, 1943' and first published that October. The fact that this happened in November 1942, but that April is twice mentioned in the text as the month when the rains are falling is a clear indication that this is far from being the whole story. Perhaps only if that black notebook comes to light shall we be able to follow in detail the strange and marvellous process of poetic creation as it struggles for the apparent inevitability of the final form.

Certain features of the southern States which Perse is to exploit in *Vents*, II, 3–4, are noticeable here and integrated into the image pattern. As the rains begin, there is 'une éclosion d'ovules d'or dans la nuit fauve des vasières' (I, 7), and the relationship between the earth's clay and the pure rain-water is explored in various ways. The poet keeps watch, 'insomnieux' (I, 11), 'insolite' (II, 2), communicating with the divine power driving the rain by the very virtue of being human clay: 'Tel s'abreuve au divin dont la lèvre est d'argile' (VII, 1). The poem itself, with 'écume aux lèvres', expresses the link between the verbal and the visual, the intellectual and the elemental. And if images of sexuality, desired or real, behind the closed shutters of the Savannah hotel are evoked as parallel cases of the violent fecundation of virgin soil, it is yet another instance of Perse seizing the opportunities that circumstances afford him.

The dangers inherent in assuming that data are directly transferred to the poem are obvious. However immediate Perse's reactions to events, he has a retentive memory—and of course a little black notebook and a vivid poetic imagination. The legal imagery in 'Pluies', such as that of the rains holding court over the town (I, 1; VIII, 1) may have been provoked by Leger's visit to a local court house where, as Ogburn recounts, he appreciated American 'shirtsleeve justice'. But one needs to recall that he took a degree in law at Bordeaux and so had a deep-seated interest in it. Another incident Ogburn mentions shows clearly how, while Perse doubtless adopted certain immediate data of his Savannah stay for 'Pluies', others were filed in his memory for later purposes. Behind the hotel was an empty swimming-pool where one night just before, believing it full of water, a girl had dived to her death. This brutal fact is elegantly transposed into the following line in *Vents*, II, 5:

> Et la Mort qui songeait dans la beauté des femmes aux terrasses, avivera ce soir d'un singulier éclat l'étoile au front de l'Etrangère, qui descend seule, après minuit, la nuit royale des sous-sols vers la piscine de turquoise illuminée d'azur.

The role of the ordering imagination is uppermost in Perse.

References to a variety of events through history and across the world—to Dido, Cortez, Aediles, the Hapsburgs, the French Revolution, a religious sect of the Middle Ages—help underline the universality of the experience Perse is trying to convey. The firm rooting of that experience in reality gives the poem a sureness of touch and a certainty of purpose which would otherwise tend to be lost, and, as the beach in 'Exil', so the rains here provide a clear basis for the imagery and a similar objective correlative for Perse's confrontation with the dark forces of poetic expression.

'Neiges': *written New York, 1943; first published Buenos Aires, 1944*
Much of the circumstantial evidence of the composition of 'Neiges' derives from the poem itself. We are told at the outset that this is the first snowfall Perse has witnessed since his arrival in America. The poet stands alone in the very early morning in his 'chambre d'angle qu'environne un Océan de neiges' (IV, 1). His temporary home is in New York, whose skyscrapers are splendidly evoked as the poet wakes to discover that snow has been falling while he slept and that the buildings now seem to be soaring skywards as all fixed points of reference have been obliterated:

> Et toute la nuit, à notre insu, sous ce haut fait de plume, portant très haut vestige et charge d'âmes, les hautes villes de pierre ponce forées d'insectes lumineux n'avaient cessé de croître et d'exceller, dans l'oubli de leur poids. (I, 2)

The optical illusion adds both dynamism to 'la fusée de marbre noir' and 'l'éperon de métal blanc' (I, 3) and a sense of unreality which is both 'songe' and 'mensonge'.

The poet's imaginary excursions to the industrial cities around the Great Lakes, to the ranches and plains of the Mid-West and on to the pine-forests where the frontiersmen continue their cold adventures (canto II); to his mother's side in occupied France (III); and into the very history of the language he is using (IV) do not present any obstacle to understanding. For however personal the recollections, they are not private: we readily comprehend and sympathise with Perse's situation and his gestures towards his host country, his mother and his chosen medium of expression.

Once we know about his exile and his grateful acceptance of real phenomena as material for his work, we are free to appreciate the subtle and powerful ways in which a literary unit has been created.

'Poème à l'Etrangère': *written Washington, D.C., and 700 acre island, Maine, 1942; first published New York, 1943*

'Exil', 'Pluies' and 'Neiges' are woven around a single central image expressing the state of exile; 'Poème à l'Etrangère' is centred rather differently on pervasive submarine imagery because it involves a second person who is herself an epitome of exile. The transposition of specific features of the U.S. capital to an underwater setting occasions different problems for the reader only insofar, firstly, as he is unfamiliar with Washington and, secondly, as they occupy a more important place in this poem than such details do in the other poems of the tetralogy. American critics, notably Knodel, have provided the necessary factual information for us not be unduly hampered by ignorance of the city. We can also rely on Perse's word: when he states something as a fact, it is so; he has no need to distort the marvels of everyday reality to integrate them into his poetry.

Yet our ultimate understanding of the poem goes well beyond the particular situation of a woman of Castilian origin exiled in Washington, and while it might be of passing interest to discover her identity, such knowledge would not increase our critical capacity in respect of the text. More relevant is the human sympathy for suffering to which the poem bears witness, all the more remarkable because only a short time before its composition Perse had found just the same difficulty of exteriorising and expressing his anguish that the Spanish lady complains of. His sympathy is thereby increased, of course, but the fact that he appears so firm a support for his friend indicates the measure of his success in turning the tables on exile.

THE IMPACT OF EXILE[8]

Crucial in that process of reversal and in our comprehension of it is the first poem of the group, but each poem indicates in various ways the triumph of Perse's courage over the forces of negation. On the sea-shore, the poet struggles in 'Exil' for his very survival as a poet. His observation, and the imagery to which it leads, is immediate and essentially local, straying only to recollect the suffering in France of those dear to him. It is the eternal voice of poetry, with whom he has a dialogue, which insists on the ubiquity and eternity of that solitude which leads to artistic expression. Perse himself is sceptical until he realises that the best way of beating the enemy is by joining him:

> ... Honore, ô Prince, ton exil!
> Et soudain tout m'est force et présence, où
> fume encore le thème du néant. ('Exil' III, 15–16)

Accepting that even when all is lost the very *act* of writing is a victory over exile, he determines to write 'un grand poème délébile' (IV, 21). What becomes of the poem afterwards is of little importance by comparison; having lost five completed works in the Gestapo raid on his Paris flat, he knows where his values lie in this respect. But he is understandably unable to continue the dynamic movement evident in *Anabase*: exile has imposed a halt upon him. So the poem seems closely bounded by the stretch of beach and the sea's horizon visible from the beach-house on Long Beach Island. Reference beyond those limits is even more closely bounded within Perse's mind, and specifically by his memories of his experiences in the Old World, in Europe and Asia. It is not, in this sense, an American poem.

Nor indeed is 'Pluies'. In it too the poet remains immobile, but the powerful deluge he describes, however much it seems to hold the town in its grip, does move slowly across. It is a tentative step from the static, and the presiding image of the poem, 'le banyan de la pluie', stresses the immobility appropriate to exile, but there is real narrative progression from the beginning to the end of the storm. It is a progression absent from 'Exil' where the principal progress made is in the crucial decision to accept the challenge of exile.

'Neiges' shows the poet again immobile but his imagination is freer to explore his adopted country now that he has begun to come to terms with his exile. Memories of France are balanced against his delighted discovery of the United States, the 3,000 miles of the continent's breadth being the counterpart to the 3,000 miles of ocean separating Perse from his homeland. One senses a gradual expansion through the poems, a development in the poet's reaction to the space about him.

Finally, in 'Poème à l'Etrangère', he is able to break free from his standing, watching posture. He can take the tram across Washington to the frame-house near the Potomac and share in another's suffering. Yet this is far from being the dynamic exploration of space which characterises the 'Etranger' of *Anabase* accompanying the nomadic tribe until it settles too permanently, too comfortably, for his restless appetencies to be satisfied. It nonetheless represents the first wary step towards the geographical dynamism of *Vents* which illustrates well that in this particular and limited respect the *Exil* tetralogy is untypical of Perse, for the poetic dynamism is exactly the same.

THE FORM OF THE POEMS

The very form of Perse's *versets* drives them relentlessly forward. Far from being unvaried, they correspond to the particular demands of the poem. In the letter to MacLeish accompanying the fair manuscript of 'Exil', Perse referred to the poem and 'ses allitérations, ses assonances et ses incantations (astreintes au rythme de la vague)'. The bracketed phrase is important: the *versets* are felt to break with the rhythmic regularity of waves on the beach where Perse stands. No two waves break in exactly the same way; no two lines of the poem have the same rhythmic effect. The interplay of incoming waves and receding wavelets has a fascinating complexity within a clear general pattern. What is more it is entirely appropriate to the narrative and imagery of the poem, revolving as they do around the shore of Long Beach Island. Motifs and images, words and sounds reverberate and interweave.

One section stands apart from the general pattern, the major part of canto vi, where the *versets* lengthen into one of Perse's great enumerations. It is a litany celebrating solitude, watchfulness and purity, registering the exceptional variety of humble tasks performed by people not reduced to ciphers by industrialisation. They are 'Princes de l'exil', an aristocracy of specialists caring for their crafts. Vigilance is the principal criterion for inclusion, and such levelling is supported by the very shaping of the text on the page. The movement of the waves is stilled in the sustained praise of Perse's fellows who fill their solitude with watchful and creative action. The poet's achievement lies in the bravely simple closing line, an *envoi* paralleled by the last lines standing apart in 'Pluies' and 'Neiges': 'Et c'est l'heure, ô Poète, de décliner ton nom, ta naissance, et ta race . . .'

There are other resemblances between the presentation of 'Pluies' and 'Exil'. Individual *versets* have sensibly similar rhythms; one canto in each dissolves the established pattern and raises the work to a climactic pitch. But in 'Pluies' the *versets* are grouped in *laisses* of three, and gradually lengthen in imitation of the heightening storm. Canto VII represents the climax of the deluge and tends towards the enumerative list in its grouping of those people and things which have to be cleansed or washed away by the action of the rains. As the rain subsides so the *versets* shorten again and resume their triple grouping until both rains and poem stop.

The blanket coverage of the snow is similarly reflected in the long stanzas or paragraphs of which the poem, with the single exception of the final line with its concentration on silence, consists. The extraordinarily high proportion of sentences starting with 'Et' emphasises the continuity and the ubiquity of the snow, the 'Epouse du monde' which clings and transforms. Of the four poems, 'Neiges' is the only one to have an apparently prose presentation.

'Poème à l'Etrangère' is the only one to have a refrain line, not exactly the same each time, as is the case in 'Récitation à l'éloge d'une Reine' and 'Amitié du Prince', but recognisably a refrain nonetheless. Otherwise, it has a consistent pattern of one long line, gradually increasing in length as the poem progresses, followed by a much shorter line whose attachment to the first is underlined by the small letter which invariably begins it. There does not appear to be any detectable imitative intention in this pattern, and in this 'Poème à l'Etrangère' is unlike its three companions, but its form is no less controlled and no less independent of traditional forms, even of those types of writing developed by *vers libristes*, by Claudel or by other writers of unrhymed poetry.

The variety of formal presentation, giving these four poems

their very different profiles, not only shows clearly how deeply concerned Perse is with the appropriate *shaping* of his poetry, but also how the impression of unity his poetry gives is created through actual diversity. In these poems he displays a thoroughly literary assimilation of the lessons of such a picture-poem as Mallarmé's *Un coup de dés*. Perse's poems are physically simpler to read, yet show no less a preoccupation with visual effect. He makes full use of the unrhymed poem's capacity for flexibility, and while eschewing the rigours of rhyme submits to other, less artificial, more dynamic demands generated from within the poem itself instead of being imposed from without. This means that the texture of Perse's language assumes a particular importance in the very structuring of the poems. The versatile system of rhythmic echoes of phrase, of word, of individual sound gives cohesion to support the interwoven patterns of imagery and narrative. Close study will reveal any number of examples, and the following will simply serve to indicate the range of Perse's use of such devices.

Firstly there are phrases which recur throughout a poem, reverberating through every fibre of its being, such as 'Et, sur toutes grèves de ce monde' in 'Exil'. After establishing it firmly almost as a refrain, Perse brilliantly expands 'Et' to 'Etranger' after the long enumeration in canto vi. The universality of exile is brought powerfully home, without any reduction in the intense feeling of personal alienation. The mysterious refrain line of 'Poème à l'Etrangère', referring to the little Paris street Rue Gît-le-cœur, functions in a similar, if more obvious, way. In 'Pluies', the opening sentence is repeated with a changed verb, 'perd' echoing 'prend', at the beginning of the penultimate section. The lines are, as it were, brackets which open and close the poem, the final canto being a kind of *envoi* after the delible poem 'qui ne fut pas écrit' (viii). Other phrases from the end of canto viii repeat or recall earlier lines: 'l'écume encore aux lèvres du poème' (cf. ii, 6), 'le beau chant que voilà sur la dissipation des eaux' (cf. i, 4, 5). But it is the 'Seigneur terrible de mon rire' who presides over the whole poem and who at the very end, as the rains and the poem stop, is dismembered by implication as the god of fair weather resumes his ascendancy: '. . . Car telles sont vos délices, *Seigneur*, au seuil aride du poème, où *mon rire* épouvante [cf. 'terrible'] les paons verts de la gloire.' What the 'Seigneur' is to 'Pluies', the 'Epouse' is to 'Neiges', gradually establishing her presence to counteract the absence of exile. As the snow espouses the earth, transforming it into a dream-like illusion ('songe' and 'mensonge'), its gentle, eminently feminine, presence makes its grace felt. The 'Epouse du monde' is in turn 'présence', 'attente' and 'prudence' to the poet alone ('Epouse du monde *ma* présence', etc.) and then, when profound sympathy has linked him with his mother, '*notre* patience' and '*notre* attente'. The rhyming (or close assonance in the case of 'attente') of the changing words serves to support the structuring force of the refrain. Other phrases at the beginning and end of the poem assert its unity while indicating the progress made: 'les grands lés tissés du songe et du réel; . . . il y eut fraîcheur de linges à nos tempes' (ɪ, ɪ) leads directly to the questioning speculation on what lies beyond (at) the end of the poem: 'Quelle navette d'os . . . nous tissera linge plus frais pour la brûlure des vivants? . . . Et au delà sont les grands lés du songe, et tout ce bien fongible où l'être engage sa fortune . . .' Similar structuring phrases complement the refrain of 'Rue Gît-le-cœur' in 'Poème à l'Etrangère': 'chantant l'hier, chantant l'ailleurs, chantant le mal à sa naissance' (ɪɪɪ, ɪ3) occurs earlier (ɪ, 9) with the slightest of differences. 'Lampes à midi' and 'à fond d'abîme' also recur and help centre both form and imagery.

Secondly there are the countless phrases repeated either immediately or very soon, usually with variations of expression within the rhythmic pattern established by its first occurrence. Sometimes whole lines are echoed in this way:

> Guerrières, ô guerrières par la lance et le trait jusqu'à nous aiguisées!
> Danseuses, ô danseuses par la danse et l'attrait au sol multipliées! ('Pluies', ɪɪɪ, 8–9)

Sometimes lines are composed partly or entirely of such meta-grammatism: 'Ah! toute chose vaine au van de la mémoire, ah! toute chose insane aux fifres de l'exil: le pur nautile des eaux libres, le pur mobile de nos songes' ('Exil', ɪᴠ, ɪ6). The technique is used for key lines to make them more memorable: 'Ma gloire est sur les sables! ma gloire est sur les sables!' ('Exil', ɪɪ, 3);

'L'exil n'est point d'hier! l'exil n'est point d'hier!' ('Exil', II, 20; VII, 6); 'Epouse du monde ma présence, épouse du monde mon attente' ('Neiges', III, 6 etc.). It allows an infinite variety not only of substitutions but also of expansions, providing both a link with what has preceded and a spring-board for new departures. The technique features most often in 'Exil', but is by no means absent from the other poems:

> A nulles rives dédiée, à nulles pages confiée la pure amorce de ce chant . . . ('Exil', II, 1)
> Et toi plus prompte sous l'éclair, ô toi plus prompte à tressaillir sur l'autre rive de son âme . . . ('Exil', VII, 4)
> De grandes nacres en croissance, de grandes nacres sans défaut méditent-elles leur réponse au plus profond des eaux? ('Neiges', II, 2)

Focussing even more closely on the text, one finds similar repetitions and substitutions at the level of individual words. Consider the parallelism of 'Et ce très haut ressac au comble de l'accès' ('Exil', III, 8). The words 'ressac' and 'l'accès', brilliantly chosen for their phonetic interplay, are supported by the semantic similarity of 'très haut' and 'comble'. The sentence 'Le ciel est un Sahel où va l'azalaïe en quête de sel gemme' ('Exil', V, 11) shows a careful accumulation of liquids and sibilants, the rare word 'l'azalaïe' with its article providing a climax in its transposition. The closing phrase of 'Pluies'—'où mon rire épouvante les paons verts de la gloire'—adds the echo by 'gloire' of 'rire' to the central metagram of 'épouvante' and 'les paons verts', in which [e], [p], [ã] and [v] are common factors. 'Chantant l'hier, chantant l'ailleurs' in 'Poème à l'Etrangère' has its similarity of sound underlined by the unusual use of the article. At every level of the text, phonic, rhythmic and semantic parallelism plays an important part, not the least of which is to guide the reader through the verbal substitutions into the image structure and so towards the poem's total significance.

PATTERNS OF IMAGERY

'Exil'

The opening line of 'Exil' is an instance of such a substitution: 'Portes ouvertes sur les sables, portes ouvertes sur l'exil'. The parallel phrasing invites the equation of 'sables' and 'l'exil' and recognition of the beach as the place of insecurity *par excellence*. One is made aware of the particular 'in-between' nature of the beach, neither truly sea nor truly land yet invested with qualities from both being formed of one by the other. It has the virtues of a threshold, at one and the same time a means of passage from one side to the other and a frontier denoting essential differences in the quality of the space to either side. The significance of the 'portes ouvertes' is consequently underlined and the reference to 'la pierre du seuil' in the next line has to be seen in relation both to the beach and to exile. The keys of the 'maison de verre', left with the lighthouse-keepers who watch and warn, are similarly connected with the idea of exile and its symbolic representation: the fact is indeed clearly stated in canto VI: 'et sur l'arène sans violence, l'exil et ses clés pures . . .' The poet's positive choice of this 'lieu flagrant et nul comme l'ossuaire des saisons' (I, 5) is largely determined by its total symbolic correspondence to his sense of deprivation and of the difficulty of reconstructing his life. Yet the refrain phrase which first appears in canto I—'Et, sur *toutes* grèves de ce monde'—indicates Perse's awareness of the universality of exile, of the communion of solitude.

His declaration of faith is bravely made in canto II: 'Ma gloire est sur les sables! ma gloire est sur les sables', and his poem is to be built on the barren treachery of 'les syrtes de l'exil', while remaining 'à nulles rives dédiée' because the poem, like the beach, is, in the poet's view, mere transience, 'fait de rien', and, as he writes later, 'délébile' (IV, 21). The recurrence of words connected with the beach—'sables', 'grèves', 'syrtes', 'rives', 'arène', and by extension 'seuil', 'lisière' etc.—makes the theme readily traceable through the poem. It is supported by reference to a temporal equivalent, 'aube', 'aurore', and by the notions of birth and creation *ex nihilo* which pervade the poem.

A generative principle in this creation, and specifically in the creation of the poem itself against all odds and Perse's own expectations, is declared in the parallel phrasing which opens the final canto: '. . . Syntaxe de l'éclair! ô pur langage de l'exil!' The intimate involvement of lightning in the poem as a principle opposite and complementary in every way to the beach begins in canto I. There 'les spasmes de l'éclair' (also perhaps the 'fers de

• •

lance') effect a 'ravissement' on the beach, and 'Exil', like Perse's lost poems, 'nés un soir à la fourche de l'éclair' (IV, 19), is 'comme ces grandes monnaies de fer exhumées par la foudre' (VI, 12). These coins had earlier been buried by the sun (V, 13) and equated with the currency of language (VI, 10). The lightning's symbolic powers of discovery, of acuity (in both literal and meta-phorical senses), provide the poet with a way forward: 'L'éclair m'ouvre le lit de plus vastes desseins. L'orage en vain déplace les bornes de l'absence' (VII, 11). Its connection with anger and passionate resentment permits the line: 'aux sables de l'exil sifflent les hautes passions lovées sous le fouet de l'éclair' (VII, 13) which ties the main threads of imagery together before the final coda.

'L'arbre de phosphore' of the lightning links sky and earth in a special way, and traditionally this is connected with the flash of insight and inspiration on the one hand and sexual penetration on the other. The ritual prostitution of Inspiration 'Partout-errante' (IV, 4; cf. VII, 9) otherwise called the 'Mendiante' (III, 14; IV, 13) is reflected in other references to sexual yet sacral relation-ships ('c'est le temps de visiter . . . le quartier des filles', VI, 6g; 'Et toi plus prompte sous l'éclair . . . parfum d'épouse dans la nuit', VII, 4–8), and in turn defines the poet's ordering role as celebrant of the rite. The intimate involvement of the poet with 'celle, la Muse, [qui n'est] pas autre que notre propre âme divinisée',[9] impinges principally, however, on his use of language. Her attributes—her seduction, her demands, her excesses, her indispensability—provide the foil for the poet to work out his problems. She provides a metaphor for his struggle to return to poetry, externalising through imagery the 'long débat' going on within him.

Her nocturnal power, eliciting from the poet, wakeful in the silence, those snatches of phrase which will eventually be moulded into poems, is one aspect of the symbolism of time in 'Exil'. Night-time is associated with the scarcely comprehensible or assimilable forces of inspiration. Dawn represents the moment of absolute purity when night and day are in perfect equilibrium. As day progresses, the poet's control increases and inspiration gives way to organisation. 'Exil' traces just such a progression, though with

2—E * *

certain cantos representing 'flash-backs', quotations, indicated as such, from the night's activity.

Canto I stands *in medias res*, being set, implicitly, in the heat of the day with silent summer lightning playing around the burning beach from which a heat-haze rises.[10] Canto II is set clearly in the morning (II, 19) and contains the first of the snatches dictated by Inspiration whose omniscience allows her a calm appraisal of the vanity of human actions. Much of canto III is taken up by her words which were spoken 'avant le jour' (III, 13), but from looking back and rejecting her advances (III, 13–15) the poet seizes on a phrase she had used and looks forward, accepting and even honouring his exile: 'Le vent nous conte sa vieillesse, le vent nous conte sa jeunesse . . . Honore, ô Prince, ton exil!' echoes 'c'est ce qu'un soir, au bord du monde, nous contèrent / Les milices du vent dans les sables d'exil . . .' (II, 13–14). The direct effect of the inner voice on the poet is shown similarly in his statement (in his own voice): 'Je reprendrai ma course de Numide' (VII, 10) which echoes her reference to 'mon âme numide' (III, 9). The intimate liaison between poet and Poetry is amply apparent. The upsurge of ideas and memories from the unconscious takes place 'chaque nuit' (III, 17) and clamours for expression 'aux premiers feux du jour' (III, 21). The idea finds full expression in canto IV, where 'l'épouse nocturne avant l'aurore reconduite' is shown out and the 'signes illicites de la nuit' removed so the quest for purity can begin at dawn. The sky 'plein d'erreurs et d'errantes prémisses' is the same in which 'l'élancement des signes les plus fastes' is noted in canto II where 'le matin pour nous mène son doigt d'augure parmi de saintes écritures' (II, 19; cf. IV, 4).

Canto V opens with part of the 'grand poème délébile' promised at the end of canto IV. The tone is personal and registers Perse's consent to the world. Midday illuminates everything, but in doing so reveals the inadequacy of appearances (V, 7–8). The sun passes its peak: after noon, 'la journée s'épaissit comme un lait' and storm clouds begin to gather, casting their shadows (V, 9, 13). The metaphor of the sun burying its treasure in the beach (V, 13) is taken up when the storm has revealed coins whose value is no longer recognised (VI, 12). Meanwhile, the enumeration of the poet's fellow 'Princes de l'exil' is a consoling reminder that the poet is not alone. In canto VII the promised storm breaks as the poet thinks of the morrow: Perse's respect for the unity of time makes one conscious of his affinities with Racinian drama.

References to time which appear literal also have metaphorical importance, then, since they point to the crucial importance for Perse of dawn. It is in this poem quite clearly the temporal equivalent to the spatial image of the beach: each is a threshold in its own dimension, a pivotal strand holding in balance the values to either side, a critical point at which everything can be dared. The spiritual and poetic potential of the threshold is greater precisely because of its precariousness. It symbolises the very function of the poet as master of mediation.

An insistence on renewal, birth and discovery is consequently found in the imagery of 'Exil'. It is linked with the fragile purity, so difficult to seize or define, of the poem and with the new life the poet is creating for himself. The doors thrown open at the outset indicate the adventure about to begin. The poet builds on the very nothingness of intangible and fleeting things, 'l'abîme et l'embrun et la fumée des sables' (ii, 6). It is a positive choice on his part to pit himself against the forces of barrenness and negation (i, 5; ii, 6). Everything in the world is new to him, including the source of his poem (ii, 21; iv, 10). The appurtenances of impurity must be burnt (iv, 18), anything that serves to mask or modify for the purposes of hypocrisy and self-deception. Only then can the poet stand naked before the ineffable simplicity of being (v, 1, 4) and take the courageous decision to fight and write on. The declaration of his 'état civil' (vii, 15) is just a first step, a certificate of re-birth.

'Pluies'

Images of renewal are even more to the forefront in 'Pluies', and the process of regeneration implied is essentially the same, working at biographical, linguistic and spiritual levels. The word 'nouveau' recurs nine times in the poem, and how many more the idea implied. The cleansing effect of rain comes to symbolise a profound purification, a ritual lustration like that effected on the threshold at the close of 'Exil', a new Flood. 'Fumées', 'scories', 'argile', 'taie', 'souillure', such are the attributes of man on earth to be washed away by the rains. As in 'Exil', language itself is one of the principal beneficiaries of this purifying process.

'Voici / La terre à fin d'usage, l'heure nouvelle dans ses langes, et mon cœur visité d'une étrange voyelle' (I, 15). The 'langue nouvelle de toutes parts offerte' (IV, 2) is likened to 'le souffle même de l'esprit', 'la chose même proférée' (IV, 3). It goes to the very heart of existence and reveals the essence. Yet this is not done with the cool superficiality of logic: Occam's razor is a bludgeon when compared with intuition and inspiration. The poem itself effervesces with 'la fraîcheur courant aux crêtes du langage' (VIII, 13; cf. II, 6), no less subject to 'unreason' than the poet confronting his muse.

The sharp penetration of inspiration and its all-embracing capacity to complement the poet's organising dominance provide the two principal patterns of imagery associated with the rains. They are at one and the same time aggressively militant and seductively feminine. They are indeed a further manifestation of the inner voice of Poetry, and Perse continues his dialogue with her throughout the poem, though this time she is entirely integrated into the central imagery, and not presented as an *alter ego*. In the early lines 'Et l'Idée nue comme un rétiaire peigne aux jardins du peuple sa crinière de fille' (I, 3), 'rétiaire' is complemented by 'fille': the nakedness appropriate to the Roman net-fighter is no less so to the girl preening herself. That 'l'Idée' refers to the rains is made clear by a later sentence: 'Les pluies vertes se peignent aux glaces des banquiers' (V, 8). Combing the hair, in primitive magic, is a part of rain-making ceremonies. The repeated phrase 'à la pointe de vos lances' (II, 5; IX, 2) continues the military image, as does the line 'L'Idée, plus nue qu'un glaive au jeu des factions' (II, 8) where the same acuity is pointed out. Yet 'l'Idée' is also 'celle qui danse comme un psylle'. The rains, likened to various female warriors in history, are then defined in their double role by two parallel *versets* (III, 8–9) where 'lance', 'trait' and 'aiguisées' in the first characterise them as 'Guerrières', and 'danse', 'attrait' and 'multipliées' in the second as 'Danseuses'. The double-edged image continues in the next line: 'Ce sont des armes à brassées, ce sont des filles par charretées . . .' The completeness assured by masculine and feminine elements engenders a sense of totality and total adequacy in the image as an instrument for exploring the source of poetic creation. The powers of destruction and fecundation are present in equal proportions: the poet determines what must be destroyed and presents his list in canto VII; the last three *laisses* of canto VIII indicate areas of gain: in the fecundation of the earth itself, in urban society where desire is reborn even in those to whom it is forbidden, and in poetic inspiration within the individual.

We have seen more than once how imperative purity is for the pursuit of the elusive multiple source of this creativity, the importance of which lies in the search for it since discovery is impossible. The purity of rain-water is used in contrast to earth and particularly mud. As the rain begins there is 'une éclosion d'ovules d'or dans la nuit fauve des vasières' (I, 7); there is 'l'argile veuve sous l'eau vierge' (I, 11), an image of purity countering barrenness which recurs in various forms. The source of the rain, for example, is said to be 'là où le ciel mûrit son goût d'arum et de névé, . . . et dans l'aubier des grandes aubes lacérées' (IV, 13–14); more perfect images of absolute purity could scarcely be imagined. The rain has to deal with routine and rottenness, self-deception and self-indulgence, mindlessness and staleness (as in the last three *laisses* of canto V). It puts everything in question: whatever preconceptions were held ('ce goût de vivre chez les hommes, . . . loin des hommes, . . . sans douceur, et voici que les Pluies . . .', V, 15; VI, 3, 12) are altered by its arrival. Through man's mask of clay (and note how he is thereby assimilated to the earth) he has the opportunity of slaking his thirst for the divine and in a totally new way with 'toute feuille lavée des signes de latrie' (VI, 14) and the conventions of worship discarded in favour of an acceptance of the elemental forces in nature.

The ritual ablution comes to a climax in canto VII. The list covers the physically active, the socially active, and written documents, each category being allotted two paragraphs. After the violent come the strong; after the (over-) careful bourgeois, the intervening social helper; after the legal documents, the purple passages. The rain has become a straightforward image of purification. Afterwards, we find 'la terre plus fraîche' (VIII, 8), no longer sterile and unfulfilled but 'la terre encore au goût de femme faite femme' (VIII, 9). However virgin the rains, they have managed to impregnate the earth and its inhabitants with a new sense of purpose.

There are relatively few evocations of lightning and the storm in general; Perse concentrates on the images immediately conjured up by his title. 'L'étincelle qui vaille' (II, 3) is none the less present and sheds light on 'la nuit claire de midi' (II, 13), the paradoxical point in time which allows the poet special insight. 'L'éclair salace' (IV, 14) reminds one of the sexual connotations mentioned in respect of the lightning in 'Exil'; here it is no less an image of the divine spark of inspiration. Here too one finds images drawn from the sea's edge and from the half-air, half-water nature of evanescent foam (I, 2; II, 6 etc.). Such threshold states provide the images which allow Perse to explore what he has given as the basic subject of the poem: '[le] ressentiment général de la condition humaine et de ses limites matérielles' (Pléiade, p. 553).

'Neiges'

'Neiges' is in some ways more accessible and certainly no less moving. As in 'Pluies', it is the title-word which declares from the outset the focal centre of the imagery, developing not only ideas traditionally or obviously associated with snow—whiteness, purity, cold, isolation, silence, fleece, feather—but also extending the range in two particular ways: religious and philological. The first is the less surprising: purity and silence invite calm and grace. Illustrating from various religious texts, Gilbert Durand, a disciple of Bachelard, underlines how 'la poétique de la neige est indicatrice d'une religion'.[11] In the same stimulating article, which strangely makes no reference to Perse's poem, one finds a helpful exploration of images linked with snow in its various guises, from individual snowflake to Alpine blizzard. But it is Perse's own, highly original, idea to make an imaginary excursion to the very source of language. It is a daring and yet essentially familiar feature to the reader of Perse's work in which language elaborated into poetry is not only the vehicle but also an integral part of both the landscape and the end in view.[12]

From the beginning of the poem, as Knodel writes in the finest study of 'Neiges' to date, 'every resource of figurative language is utilized to make the sight, feel, and sound of snow more vivid to the reader'.[13] The *texture* of snow (and note the word's Latin etymon shared with both *text* and *textile*), 'une fraîcheur de *linges* à nos tempes' as it falls 'sur les grands *lés tissés* du songe et du réel' (I, 1; my italics), is immediately conjured up and linked with themes to be developed: 'un havre de fortune'—the precarious sense of exile; 'un lieu de grâce et de merci'—the religious imagery of canto III; 'l'essaim des grandes odes du silence'— the *Ursprache* of canto IV, the unspoken force behind so many actual languages. In the windless grey dawn muffling the city, skyscrapers with the occasional lighted window appear to be soaring upwards in the optical illusion created by the falling snow. A sense of weightlessness, of detachment from the earth, continues the radical sense of transfiguration. The ineffable gentleness of the snow is beyond human knowledge, not only in the immediate sense that it began to fall when everyone was sleeping but also because such purity defies analysis: only the purest imagination does not defile it:

Nul n'a surpris, nul n'a connu, au plus haut front de pierre, le premier affleurement de cette heure soyeuse, le premier attouchement de cette chose fragile et très futile, comme un frôlement de cils. ('Neiges' I, 3)

The exquisitely expressive visual image—'l'aube muette dans sa plume, comme une grande chouette fabuleuse en proie aux souffles de l'esprit, enflait son corps de dahlia blanc' (I, 4)— continues the sense of growth of wonder, of the texture and pervasive beauty of the snow.

Canto I sets the scene; the other three cantos form, as it were, a clover-leaf pattern around that centre, branching out in different directions yet remaining firmly within the orbit determined by the crystallising image of the snow, even, one might say, reflecting the hexagonal form of an ice-crystal. From the gulf and estuary of the St Lawrence, canto II moves in the poet's imagination upstream to the Niagara Falls and the Great Lakes. From there he projects westward across the plains and ranches to the coniferous forests where the frontiersman still hunts for a living. And everywhere there is snow, its attributes changing according to circumstance. At sea it is 'ce naissain pâle'; over city stations 'la nuit laiteuse engendre une fête de gui'; factory lighting consists of 'mille lampes choyées des choses grèges de la neige' and these are reflected in the lake as 'de grandes nacres sans défaut . . . au plus profond des eaux'; on industrial slagheaps it is 'neige plus fine qu'au désert la graine de coriandre, neige plus fraîche qu'en avril le premier lait des jeunes bêtes . . .' Its essential whiteness and the misty ubiquity of its presence at dawn is underscored through dozens of references: echoing a title of Gautier's one could call it a 'symphonie en blanc mineur'. And 'la blancheur', as Durand notes, 'est l'équivalent plastique du silence'.[14] From there to a sense of absence is but a short step.

It is this that comes out most forcibly in canto III. A phrase from the beginning of the poem—'les premières neiges de l'absence'—is caught up for expansion with particular reference to the poet's mother, to whom 'Neiges' is dedicated. The purity and grace of the snow is seen in her and associated with the religious beliefs which her son does not share but which give her strength in such difficult times in France. The 'langage sans paroles' which mother and son understand is a variant of the 'grandes odes du silence' (I, 1) and of the *Ursprache* soon to appear. 'Cette affre de douceur' is similarly an equivalent to the bitter-sweet arrival of the snow (cf. 'inquiétante douceur', II, 4), and expresses well the paradox of Perse's situation in exile: an absent presence. His mother's silent vigil matches his own in its transcendence of suffering, and each is imaged in the transfiguration which the snow effects upon the earth. Hence the multiplicity of significance in the refrain 'Epouse du monde ma présence, épouse du monde mon attente', which reverberates through the poem like an echoing greeting. Recognition of his own lineage leads Perse to think of his origins, and just as canto II takes us literally upstream towards the frontiers of the unknown, so another quest for origins takes us up another stream in canto IV. The 'eaux premières' (IV, 2) of the mother's womb and of original chaos are no less those in which language is born, and indeed language and life are synonymous for the poet.

The world of appearances—'les vertes apparences' (IV, 1)—is left behind in favour of a deeper and purer reality, where 'une âme non guéable' (IV, 5) enjoys 'un lieu de grâce et de merci pour la montée des sûrs présages de l'esprit' (IV, 4; cf. I, 1). On the threshold of day the poet stands '[au] seuil de la connaissance! avant-seuil de l'éclat!' (*Amers*, Strophe, II). 'Cet éclat sévère où toute langue perd ses armes' ('Neiges', IV, 1) is just the revelation of the real presence underlying absence enjoyed by 'ceux-là qui, de naissance, tiennent leur connaissance au-dessus du savoir' (*Amers*, Invocation, 6).[15]

Images of weaving and fabrics, of language and religion, of purity and grace, of mistiness and illusion are all facets of the crystalline blanket of snow. Beyond the immediate and imagined snowscape, beyond the delicacy of feeling for his mother, beyond even the quest for the source of language is the metaphysical question about the nature of reality. 'Il y a une réalité du songe et du mensonge qui vaut bien celle de la réalité objective.' Durand's remark, based on his own 'psychanalyse de la neige', is extraordinarily close to some of Perse's observations:

> Epouse du monde ma présence, épouse du monde mon attente! Que nous ravisse encore la fraîche haleine de mensonge! ... ('Neiges' III, 6)

The fact of the snow—'ce haut fait de plume' (1, 2)—transforms the facts of urban and other phenomena. Yet the purification is transient, establishing as a temporary truth something that is in fact a lie. For Perse his poem is no less transient; it too is an illusion, a fiction created from a common fund of words. The image of the snow is intimately linked, therefore, with Perse's view of language; the philological excursion towards the *Ursprache* is integral to the sense of the poem in this fundamental way. In 'Pluies' (V, 7), Perse writes of the 'fade saison de l'homme sans méprise', another way of suggesting that much of life's piquancy lies in illusion. Similarly much of the magic of the repeated 'Rue Gît-le-cœur' in 'Poème à l'Etrangère' stems from the fact that it is uttered by various mistaken exiles—'et ce sont là méprises de leur langue d'étrangères' (II, 13). It becomes clear that for all Perse's attachment to natural phenomena and to excellence in human activity, he is well aware that these are not ends in themselves. Self-satisfaction in whatever field is heartily condemned, not in a way that will cause offence to the self-satisfied—'la politesse n'est-elle pas encore la meilleure formule de liberté?'—so much as in a way that leaves Perse complete freedom of thought and action. And that freedom is precisely the reverse side of the coin of the sense of exile.

'Poème à l'Etrangère'

The first three poems of the tetralogy are structured around the nucleus of an objective correlative of exile. Beach, rain and snow in turn reflect the sense of precariousness imposed by exile, and through his exploration of them as images subtending the narrative, the poet makes a fundamental reassessment of values, probing deeply into the nature of man, of reality and of language in relation to both. His explicit or implicit dialogue involving Poet and Poetry centres on a down-to-earth object, sufficiently familiar and universal for his metaphysical speculations to remain poetry rather than become philosophy, yet involving both. This bifocal vision of both particular and universal, concrete and abstract, is equally apparent in 'Poème à l'Etrangère', but there the use of imagery is rather different, since the Etrangère is a personal embodiment of exile, and imagery based on objects plays a subsidiary role.

The Etrangère is an individual, yet comes across as a type, a symbol of the struggle which Perse himself had to tackle. She serves to exteriorise his own problems and see them more objectively through the very assistance he offers her. The dialogue takes place on a Washington stage between two human actors specifically French and Spanish in origin rather than, as in 'Exil', between one human and one 'divine' protagonist, and such specification in itself tends to limit the scope of the poem and make it the most 'occasional' of the four. The particular setting intrudes far more here and even the supporting 'submarine' imagery depends, one gathers from American critics, on a particular quality of light in the late summer atmosphere hanging heavy around the Potomac river. Such particularity is not in itself a fault, indeed we have seen how Perse's poems always stem from a particular set of circumstances, but the setting of 'Poème à l'Etrangère' does not lend itself so readily to universal comprehension as do beach, rainstorm and snowfall.

This is not to say that the underwater imagery of the poem does not become another symbol of exile. The sense of being at one remove, in a strange and unnatural environment, comes across strongly. The frame-house in the humid greenery of the Potomac valley, ambiguously 'à fond d'abîme' (literally 'bottomless' but in Perse's syntax 'in the depths'), 'mûrit un fruit de lampes à midi' (I, 3) in its attempt to achieve the 'nuit claire de midi' of 'Pluies' (II, 13). The effort leads instead to 'de plus tièdes couvaisons de souffrances nouvelles' (I, 4) for the Etrangère, differentiating her absorption in despair from Perse's own, more courageous, confrontation of exile. He, from his Washington *pied-à-terre*, follows the tramlines towards the underwater 'pays des Atlantes' past other features of the capital which in the poet's imagination have been overrun by water:

> 'par les . . . ronds-points d'Observatoires envahis de sar-gasses,
> par les quartiers d'eaux vives . . . par les quartiers de Nègres et d'Asiates aux migrations d'alevins, et par les beaux solstices verts des places rondes comme des attolls,
> (là où campait un soir la cavalerie des Fédéraux, ô mille têtes d'hippocampes!) ('Poème à l'Etrangère' I, 6–8)

The Etrangère's incapacity to surmount her difficulties is voiced as a plea to the poet in canto II: 'vous qui chantez tous bannissements au monde, ne me chanterez-vous pas un chant du soir à la mesure de mon mal?' (II, 5). Her hope is to escape from 'tout ce bruit des grandes eaux que fait la nuit du Nouveau Monde' (II, 4) and return to her natural element: the imagery accordingly shifts to the aerial, to bells and the flight and song of birds. In her confusion she is blind to the wonders the poet sees around him and refuses to listen to the compensations such awareness brings.

The poet's sympathy is therefore extended in a direction she is more likely to appreciate. In his answer to her plea, in canto III, he takes the submarine imagery and shows its positive aspects and the way in which an optimistic and creative attitude can turn the tables on despair. The hard-won lesson of 'Exil' has been well learnt and is now offered for the benefit of one who unwisely felt she could escape by shutting herself off from the world. Her closed shutters, sleepless nights and drugging cigars are no substitute for optimism and open eyes. For Perse, 'comme un nid de Sibylles, l'abîme enfante ses merveilles: lucioles!' (III, 4). Oracles, marvels, fireflies! All three are linked in the poet's mind with the whole process of poetic creation. The enigma of inspiration combines with natural wonders in the formation of the poem, and the fireflies seem a symbol of the processes of intellection involved in its writing. So the poet goes 'lauré d'abeilles de phosphore, ... sifflant [son] peuple de Sibylles' (III, 17) as the poem nears completion. The fireflies replace the 'cigales mortes d'un Eté' flushed downstream, and a new value is attached to the 'bruit de grandes eaux':

> par les tuyauteries des chambres, montant des fosses atlan-
> tides, avec ce goût de l'incréé comme une haleine d'outremonde,
> c'est un parfum d'abîme et de néant parmi les moisissures de
> la terre ... ('Poème à l'Etrangère' III, 7–8)

However negative 'abîme' and 'néant' may appear, one recalls Perse's reversal of their values in 'Exil'; they are not invincible: 'J'ai fondé sur l'abîme', 'Et soudain tout m'est force et présence où fume encore le thème du néant' ('Exil', II, 6; III, 16). 'L'incréé' has to be given form, 'une haleine d'outre-monde' breathed in deeply when the opportunity is offered. Where the Etrangère had seen only hostility, Perse sees creative potential: the act of poetry is a redemptive power. It is this message common to all four poems that links 'Poème à l'Etrangère' securely to the rest of the tetralogy. It presents a different view of exile, inevitably over-lapping with, but also complementary to the aspects explored in 'Exil', 'Pluies' and 'Neiges'.

THE LANGUAGE OF EXILE

It can scarcely have gone unnoticed that at every turn, in different guises, looms the question of language. It is the means by which the poet fills the great gulf of exile, and its wealth of vocabulary, syntax, phonetic texture and poetic devices using all three is an integral part of the reversal process. The thrust towards ever new frontiers that is a hallmark of Perse's poetry is diverted by the circumstances of exile into an introspective search for the sources of poetry and a justification, for himself as much as (if not more than) for us, of its vital currents. Yet Perse's lan-guage is never simply self-regarding: meaning is not sacrificed to the verbal music, nor are words the sole end of the poetry.

It might seem that *Exil*, being the result of an imposition, is unrepresentative of Perse. Nothing, I suggest, could be further from the truth. He himself has called it 'un poème de l'éternité de l'exil dans la condition humaine' (Pléiade, p. 576). The profound awareness of man's fundamental solitude is variously expressed in all Perse's poems, which show different ways of coming to terms with such a sense of exile. Initially, then, is the awareness, born of depths which one may leave to psychoanalysts to probe. This awareness, compounded with the geographical removes which we know from Perse's biography, led to a choice, that of becoming a career diplomat or, as Claudel put it, 'le professionnel de l'absence'.[16] Perse was in many respects prepared for exile, had, so to speak, a natural vocation for it, and the circumstances of his political exile coincided with certain deep inclinations in him which are apparent in all the earlier poems. The exiled Crusoe, the Prince in the solitude of his authority, the nomadic Etranger of *Anabase* all reflect Perse's profound sense of exile. It is in this way that *Exil* expresses more fully his real nature, his total self, than any other of his works. The subsequent poems continue to a large degree the dialectic of exile, stressing the positive pole. But a positive is positive only in relation to a negative: in *Exil* both poles are in view and in the balance. The tetralogy consequently stands at the crossroads of Perse's output, at another threshold allowing especial penetration: 'l'exil et ses clés pures' is a crucial key to his whole work.

While *Exil* might seem, to some more than to others, to have particular significance when applied to the circumstances of World War II, it has far less affinities with French Resistance poetry of the time, whether written in France by Aragon, Cassou, Eluard or Char, or abroad by Jouve or Supervielle, than with the great poems of literal and metaphysical exile sung in the Pentateuch or by Job, Homer, Virgil, Ovid, Dante or Milton. The similarity, however, is in the underlying eternal theme, the 'langage' of exile; if there are specific verbal echoes at the level of 'la langue', they derive from the common concern and the inevitable use of a common fund of language and imagery and not from any desire on Perse's part to present literary echoes. The kind of notes that Eliot appended to 'The Waste Land' are totally foreign to Perse's poetics. His poems reach towards the quality of epic without the benefit of a pre-established basis of history or legend, and yet, in this age of the individual, and hence of the uncommunicable, approach the status of myth in its fundamental, universal applicability. Even Perse's use of a pseudonym is partly in recognition of his mythopœic aim for anonymity, for the expression of the universal behind and beyond the particular.

Yet Perse's highly individual style speaks at every turn of a single articulating mind, one which painstakingly organises every aspect of the poems. However closed to the analysis of discursive reason the inspirational source of each poem, one can trace through the imagery and the narrative shaping the guiding hand of the poet. Nothing is random: the interaction of dawn between the dark night of intuition and the clear light of logic leads to some marvellous insights taking advantage of both. It is ultimately this openness on Perse's part, this preparedness to accept every experience of the mind and the senses, that is perhaps most inspiring. For while so many poets, writing of poetry in inbred poems, indulge in a kind of mental masturbation, Perse relishes his keen perception of real phenomena and relates his *ars poetica* intimately to timeless themes and images drawn from outside the literary experience. He sees the poet's task as one of clarification, not so much of natural phenomena, which are there for those that have senses to perceive, as of man's relationship to them and to the scarcely explored world of his own psyche. These are vital matters for man at large, not simply for the devotee of poetry.

I hope I have shown, and hope to show further on points of detail in the notes, that by considering the general circumstances in which *Exil* was written and various aspects of the text itself, its narrative and implications, its thematic structures and poetic construction, there are multiple approaches contributing both to comprehension and a just appraisal. The reader will find, I believe, that his reward is in exponential proportion to his effort. If there are insoluble problems, by definition always the most interesting ones, he may care to recall a sentence from Perse's Nobel Prize speech when he said of poetry: 'L'obscurité qu'on lui reproche ne tient pas à sa nature propre, qui est d'éclairer, mais à la nuit même qu'elle explore, et qu'elle se doit d'explorer: celle de l'âme elle-même et du mystère où baigne l'être humain.'

E X I L

A Archibald MacLeish

I

    *Portes ouvertes sur les sables, portes ouvertes
sur l'exil,*

    *Les clés aux gens du phare, et l'astre roué vif
sur la pierre du seuil :*

    *Mon hôte, laissez-moi votre maison de verre
dans les sables . . .*

    *L'Été de gypse aiguise ses fers de lance dans
nos plaies,*

    J'élis un lieu flagrant et nul comme l'ossuaire   5
des saisons,

    *Et, sur toutes grèves de ce monde, l'esprit du
dieu fumant déserte sa couche d'amiante.*

    *Les spasmes de l'éclair sont pour le ravissement
des Princes en Tauride.*

II

A nulles rives dédiée, à nulles pages confiée
la pure amorce de ce chant . . .
        D'autres saisissent dans les temples la corne
peinte des autels :
        Ma gloire est sur les sables ! ma gloire est sur
les sables ! . . . Et ce n'est point errer, ô Pérégrin,
        Que de convoiter l'aire la plus nue pour assem-
bler aux syrtes de l'exil un grand poème né de rien,
un grand poème fait de rien . . .
        Sifflez, ô frondes par le monde, chantez, ô   5
conques sur les eaux !
        J'ai fondé sur l'abîme et l'embrun et la fumée
des sables. Je me coucherai dans les citernes et dans
les vaisseaux creux,
        En tous lieux vains et fades où gît le goût de
la grandeur.

        « . . . Moins de souffles flattaient la famille des
Jules ; moins d'alliances assistaient les grandes
castes de prêtrise.
        Où vont les sables à leur chant s'en vont les
Princes de l'exil,
        Où furent les voiles haut tendues s'en va l'épave   10
plus soyeuse qu'un songe de luthier,
        Où furent les grandes actions de guerre déjà
blanchit la mâchoire d'âne,
        Et la mer à la ronde roule son bruit de crânes
sur les grèves,
        Et que toutes choses au monde lui soient vaines,
c'est ce qu'un soir, au bord du monde, nous contèrent
        Les milices du vent dans les sables d'exil . . . »

        Sagesse de l'écume, ô pestilences de l'esprit   15
dans la crépitation du sel et le lait de chaux vive !

Une science m'échoit aux sévices de l'âme...
Le vent nous conte ses flibustes, le vent nous conte
ses méprises!

Comme le Cavalier, la corde au poing, à
l'entrée du désert,

J'épie au cirque le plus vaste l'élancement des
signes les plus fastes.

Et le matin pour nous mène son doigt d'augure
parmi de saintes écritures.

L'exil n'est point d'hier! l'exil n'est point   20
d'hier! « Ô vestiges, ô prémisses »,

Dit l'Étranger parmi les sables, « toute chose
au monde m'est nouvelle!...» Et la naissance de
son chant ne lui est pas moins étrangère.

III

« ...Toujours il y eut cette clameur, toujours il y eut cette splendeur,

Et comme un haut fait d'armes en marche par le monde, comme un dénombrement de peuples en exode, comme une fondation d'empires par tumulte prétorien, ha! comme un gonflement de lèvres sur la naissance des grands Livres,

Cette grande chose sourde par le monde et qui s'accroît soudain comme une ébriété.

« ...Toujours il y eut cette clameur, toujours il y eut cette grandeur,

Cette chose errante par le monde, cette haute transe par le monde, et sur toutes grèves de ce monde, du même souffle proférée, la même vague proférant

Une seule et longue phrase sans césure à jamais inintelligible...

« ...Toujours il y eut cette clameur, toujours il y eut cette fureur,

Et ce très haut ressac au comble de l'accès, toujours, au faîte du désir, la même mouette sur son aile, la même mouette sur son aire, à tire-d'aile ralliant les stances de l'exil, et sur toutes grèves de ce monde, du même souffle proférée, la même plainte sans mesure

A la poursuite, sur les sables, de mon âme numide... »

Je vous connais, ô monstre! Nous voici de nouveau face à face. Nous reprenons ce long débat où nous l'avions laissé.

Et vous pouvez pousser vos arguments comme des mufles bas sur l'eau : je ne vous laisserai point de pause ni répit.

Sur trop de grèves visitées furent mes pas lavés avant le jour, sur trop de couches désertées fut mon âme livrée au cancer du silence.

Que voulez-vous encore de moi, ô souffle originel? Et vous, que pensez-vous encore tirer de ma lèvre vivante,

Ô force errante sur mon seuil, ô Mendiante dans nos voies et sur les traces du Prodigue?

Le vent nous conte sa vieillesse, le vent nous conte sa jeunesse... Honore, ô Prince, ton exil!

Et soudain tout m'est force et présence, où fume encore le thème du néant.

« ... Plus haute, chaque nuit, cette clameur muette sur mon seuil, plus haute, chaque nuit, cette levée de siècles sous l'écaille,

Et, sur toutes grèves de ce monde, un ïambe plus farouche à nourrir de mon être!...

Tant de hauteur n'épuisera la rive accore de ton seuil, ô Saisisseur de glaives à l'aurore,

Ô Manieur d'aigles par leurs angles, et Nourrisseur des filles les plus aigres sous la plume de fer!

Toute chose à naître s'horripile à l'orient du monde, toute chair naissante exulte aux premiers feux du jour!

Et voici qu'il s'élève une rumeur plus vaste par le monde, comme une insurrection de l'âme...

Tu ne te tairas point, clameur! que je n'aie dépouillé sur les sables toute allégeance humaine. (Qui sait encore le lieu de ma naissance?) »

IV

Étrange fut la nuit où tant de souffles s'éga-
rèrent au carrefour des chambres . . .

Et qui donc avant l'aube erre aux confins du
monde avec ce cri pour moi? Quelle grande fille
répudiée s'en fut au sifflement de l'aile visiter d'autres
seuils, quelle grande fille malaimée,

A l'heure où les constellations labiles qui
changent de vocable pour les hommes d'exil déclinent
dans les sables à la recherche d'un lieu pur?

Partout-errante fut son nom de courtisane chez
les prêtres, aux grottes vertes des Sibylles, et le matin
sur notre seuil sut effacer les traces de pieds nus,
parmi de saintes écritures . . .

Servantes, vous serviez, et vaines, vous tendiez   5
vos toiles fraîches pour l'échéance d'un mot pur.

Sur des plaintes de pluviers s'en fut l'aube
plaintive, s'en fut l'hyade pluvieuse à la recherche
du mot pur,

Et sur les rives très anciennes fut appelé mon
nom . . . L'esprit du dieu fumait parmi les cendres de
l'inceste.

Et quand se fut parmi les sables essorée la
substance pâle de ce jour,

De beaux fragments d'histoires en dérive, sur
des pales d'hélices, dans le ciel plein d'erreurs et
d'errantes prémisses, se mirent à virer pour le délice
du scoliaste.

Et qui donc était là qui s'en fut sur son aile?   10
Et qui donc, cette nuit, a sur ma lèvre d'étranger
pris encore malgré moi l'usage de ce chant?

Renverse, ô scribe, sur la table des grèves, du
revers de ton style la cire empreinte du mot vain.

Les eaux du large laveront, les eaux du large
sur nos tables, les plus beaux chiffres de l'année.

Et c'est l'heure, ô Mendiante, où sur la face close des grands miroirs de pierre exposés dans les antres

L'officiant chaussé de feutre et ganté de soie grège efface, à grand renfort de manches, l'affleurement des signes illicites de la nuit.

Ainsi va toute chair au cilice du sel, le fruit de cendre de nos veilles, la rose naine de vos sables, et l'épouse nocturne avant l'aurore reconduite . . .   15

Ah! toute chose vaine au van de la mémoire, ah! toute chose insane aux fifres de l'exil : le pur nautile des eaux libres, le pur mobile de nos songes,

Et les poèmes de la nuit avant l'aurore répudiés, l'aile fossile prise au piège des grandes vêpres d'ambre jaune . . .

Ah! qu'on brûle, ah! qu'on brûle, à la pointe des sables, tout ce débris de plume, d'ongle, de chevelures peintes et de toiles impures,

Et les poèmes nés d'hier, ah! les poèmes nés un soir à la fourche de l'éclair, il en est comme de la cendre au lait des femmes, trace infime . . .

Et de toute chose ailée dont vous n'avez usage,   20
me composant un pur langage sans office,

Voici que j'ai dessein encore d'un grand poème délébile . . .

V

« *. . .Comme celui qui se dévêt à la vue de la mer, comme celui qui s'est levé pour honorer la première brise de terre (et voici que son front a grandi sous le casque),*

Les mains plus nues qu'à ma naissance et la lèvre plus libre, l'oreille à ces coraux où gît la plainte d'un autre âge,

Me voici restitué à ma rive natale . . . Il n'est d'histoire que de l'âme, il n'est d'aisance que de l'âme.

Avec l'achaine, l'anophèle, avec les chaumes et les sables, avec les choses les plus frêles, avec les choses les plus vaines, la simple chose, la simple chose que voilà, la simple chose d'être là, dans l'écoulement du jour . . .

Sur des squelettes d'oiseaux nains s'en va l'enfance de ce jour, en vêtement des îles, et plus légère que l'enfance sur ses os creux de mouette, de guifette, la brise enchante les eaux filles en vêtement d'écailles pour les îles . . . 5

Ô sables, ô résines! l'élytre pourpre du destin dans une grande fixité de l'œil! et sur l'arène sans violence, l'exil et ses clés pures, la journée traversée d'un os vert comme un poisson des îles . . .

Midi chante, ô tristesse! . . . et la merveille est annoncée par ce cri : ô merveille! et ce n'est pas assez d'en rire sous les larmes . . .

Mais qu'est-ce là, oh! qu'est-ce, en toute chose, qui soudain fait défaut? . . . »

Je sais. J'ai vu. Nul n'en convienne! — Et déjà la journée s'épaissit comme un lait.

L'ennui cherche son ombre aux royaumes d'Arsace: et la tristesse errante mène son goût 10 d'euphorbe par le monde, l'espace où vivent les rapaces tombe en d'étranges déshérences . . .

Plaise au sage d'épier la naissance des schismes!. . . Le ciel est un Sahel où va l'azalaïe en quête de sel gemme.

Plus d'un siècle se voile aux défaillances de l'histoire.

Et le soleil enfouit ses beaux sesterces dans les sables, à la montée des ombres où mûrissent les sentences d'orage.

Ô présides sous l'eau verte! qu'une herbe illustre sous les mers nous parle encore de l'exil . . . et le Poète prend ombrage

De ces grandes feuilles de calcaire, à fleur d'abîme, sur des socles : dentelle au masque de la mort . . .

VI

« . . .*Celui qui erre, à la mi-nuit, sur les gale-*   1a
ries de pierre pour estimer les titres d'une belle
comète; celui qui veille, entre deux guerres, à la pureté   b
des grandes lentilles de cristal; celui qui s'est levé   c
avant le jour pour curer les fontaines, et c'est la fin
des grandes épidémies; celui qui laque en haute mer   d
avec ses filles et ses brus, et c'en était assez des cendres
de la terre . . .

Celui qui flatte la démence aux grands hospices   2a
de craie bleue, et c'est Dimanche sur les seigles, à
l'heure de grande cécité; celui qui monte aux orgues   b
solitaires, à l'entrée des armées; celui qui rêve un   c
jour d'étranges latomies, et c'est un peu après midi,
à l'heure de grande viduité; celui qu'éveille en mer,   d
sous le vent d'une île basse, le parfum de sécheresse
d'une petite immortelle des sables; celui qui veille,   e
dans les ports, aux bras des femmes d'autre race,
et c'est un goût de vétiver dans le parfum d'aisselle
de la nuit basse, et c'est un peu après minuit, à
l'heure de grande opacité; celui, dans le sommeil,   f
dont le souffle est relié au souffle de la mer, et au
renversement de la marée voici qu'il se retourne sur
sa couche comme un vaisseau change d'amures . . .

Celui qui peint l'amer au front des plus hauts   3a
caps, celui qui marque d'une croix blanche la face
des récifs; celui qui lave d'un lait pauvre les grandes   b
casemates d'ombre au pied des sémaphores, et c'est
un lieu de cinéraires et de gravats pour la délectation
du sage; celui qui prend logement, pour la saison   c
des pluies, avec les gens de pilotage et de bornage —
chez le gardien d'un temple mort à bout de péninsule
(et c'est sur un éperon de pierre gris-bleu, ou sur
la haute table de grès rouge); celui qu'enchaîne,   d
sur les cartes, la course close des cyclones; pour qui   e

s'éclairent, aux nuits d'hiver, les grandes pistes f
sidérales; ou qui démêle en songe bien d'autres lois
de transhumance et de dérivation; celui qui quête, g
à bout de sonde, l'argile rouge des grands fonds pour
modeler la face de son rêve; celui qui s'offre, dans h
les ports, à compenser les boussoles pour la marine
de plaisance . . .

    Celui qui marche sur la terre à la rencontre des 4a
grands lieux d'herbe; qui donne, sur sa route, consul- b
tation pour le traitement d'un très vieil arbre; celui c
qui monte aux tours de fer, après l'orage, pour éventer
ce goût de crêpe sombre des feux de ronces en forêt;
celui qui veille, en lieux stériles, au sort des grandes d
lignes télégraphiques; qui sait le gîte et la culée e
d'atterrissage des maîtres câbles sous-marins; qui f
soigne sous la ville, en lieu d'ossuaires et d'égouts
(et c'est à même l'écorce démasclée de la terre), les
instruments lecteurs de purs séismes . . .

    Celui qui a la charge, en temps d'invasion, 5a
du régime des eaux, et fait visite aux grands bassins
filtrants lassés des noces d'éphémères; celui qui garde b
de l'émeute, derrière les ferronneries d'or vert, les
grandes serres fétides du Jardin Botanique; les c
grands Offices des Monnaies, des Longitudes et des
Tabacs; et le Dépôt des Phares, où gisent les fables, d
les lanternes; celui qui fait sa ronde, en temps de e
siège, aux grands halls où s'émiettent, sous verre,
les panoplies de phasmes, de vanesses; et porte sa f
lampe aux belles auges de lapis, où, friable, la prin-
cesse d'os épinglée d'or descend le cours des siècles
sous sa chevelure de sisal; celui qui sauve des armées g
un hybride très rare de rosier-ronce hymalayen; celui h
qui entretient de ses deniers, aux grandes banque-
routes de l'État, le luxe trouble des haras, des grands
haras de brique fauve sous les feuilles, comme des
roseraies de roses rouges sous les roucoulements
d'orage, comme de beaux gynécées pleins de princes
sauvages, de ténèbres, d'encens et de substance mâle . . .
    Celui qui règle, en temps de crise, le gardiennage 6a

*des hauts paquebots mis sous scellés, à la boucle
d'un fleuve couleur d'iode, de purin (et sous le limbe
des verrières, aux grands salons bâchés d'oubli,
c'est une lumière d'agave pour les siècles et à jamais
vigile en mer); celui qui vaque, avec les gens de*   b
*peu, sur les chantiers et sur les cales désertées par
la foule, après le lancement d'une grande coque de
trois ans; celui qui a pour profession d'agréer les*   c
navires; et celui-là qui trouve un jour le parfum de   d
son âme dans le vaigrage d'un voilier neuf; celui   e
*qui prend la garde d'équinoxe sur le rempart des
docks, sur le haut peigne sonore des grands barrages
de montagne, et sur les grandes écluses océanes;
celui, soudain, pour qui s'exhale toute l'haleine
incurable de ce monde dans le relent des grands silos
et entrepôts de denrées coloniales, là où l'épice et le
grain vert s'enflent aux lunes d'hivernage comme la
création sur son lit fade; celui qui prononce la clôture*   g
*des grands congrès d'orographie, de climatologie,
et c'est le temps de visiter l'Arboretum et l'Aquarium
et le quartier des filles, les tailleries de pierres fines
et le parvis des grands convulsionnaires . . .*

     Celui qui ouvre un compte en banque pour les   7a
recherches de l'esprit; celui qui entre au cirque de   b
*son œuvre nouvelle dans une très grande animation
de l'être, et, de trois jours, nul n'a regard sur son
silence que sa mère, nul n'a l'accès de sa chambre
que la plus vieille des servantes; celui qui mène aux*   c
sources sa monture sans y boire lui-même; celui   d
*qui rêve, aux selleries, d'un parfum plus ardent
que celui de la cire; celui, comme Baber, qui vêt la*   e
*robe du poète entre deux grandes actions viriles pour
révérer la face d'une belle terrasse; celui qui tombe*   f
*en distraction pendant la dédicace d'une nef, et au
tympan sont telles cruches, comme des ouïes, murées
pour l'acoustique; celui qui tient en héritage, sur*   g
*terre de main-morte, la dernière héronnière, avec de
beaux ouvrages de vénerie, de fauconnerie; celui*   h
qui tient commerce, en ville, de très grands livres :

almagestes, portulans et bestiaires; qui prend souci   j
des accidents de phonétique, de l'altération des signes
et des grandes érosions du langage; qui participe   k
aux grands débats de sémantique; qui fait autorité   m
dans les mathématiques usuelles et se complaît à la
supputation des temps pour le calendrier des fêtes
mobiles (le nombre d'or, l'indiction romaine, l'épacte
et les grandes lettres dominicales); celui qui donne   n
la hiérarchie aux grands offices du langage; celui   p
à qui l'on montre, en très haut lieu, de grandes
pierres lustrées par l'insistance de la flamme . . .

    Ceux-là sont princes de l'exil et n'ont que faire   8
de mon chant. »

    Étranger, sur toutes grèves de ce monde, sans
audience ni témoin, porte à l'oreille du Ponant une
conque sans mémoire :
    Hôte précaire à la lisière de nos villes, tu ne   10
franchiras point le seuil des Lloyds, où ta parole
n'a point cours et ton or est sans titre . . .
    « *J'habiterai mon nom* », *fut ta réponse aux*
questionnaires du port. Et sur les tables du changeur,
tu n'as rien que de trouble à produire,
    Comme ces grandes monnaies de fer exhumées
par la foudre.

VII

« . . .*Syntaxe de l'éclair! ô pur langage de l'exil!
Lointaine est l'autre rive où le message s'illumine:*

    *Deux fronts de femmes sous la cendre, du même
pouce visités; deux ailes de femmes aux persiennes,
du même souffle suscitées . . .*

    *Dormiez-vous cette nuit, sous le grand arbre
de phosphore, ô cœur d'orante par le monde, ô mère
du Proscrit, quand dans les glaces de la chambre
fut imprimée sa face?*

    *Et toi plus prompte sous l'éclair, ô toi plus
prompte à tressaillir sur l'autre rive de son âme,
compagne de sa force et faiblesse de sa force, toi dont
le souffle au sien fut à jamais mêlé,*

    *T'assiéras-tu encore sur sa couche déserte, dans
le hérissement de ton âme de femme?*   5

    *L'exil n'est point d'hier! l'exil n'est point
d'hier! . . . Exècre, ô femme, sous ton toit un chant
d'oiseau de Barbarie . . .*

    *Tu n'écouteras point l'orage au loin multiplier
la course de nos pas sans que ton cri de femme, dans
la nuit, n'assaille encore sur son aire l'aigle équivoque
du bonheur!* »

    . . .*Tais-toi, faiblesse, et toi, parfum d'épouse
dans la nuit comme l'amande même de la nuit.*

    *Partout errante sur les grèves, partout errante
sur les mers, tais-toi, douceur, et toi présence gréée
d'ailes à hauteur de ma selle.*

    Je reprendrai ma course de Numide, longeant   10
*la mer inaliénable . . . Nulle verveine aux lèvres, mais
sur la langue encore, comme un sel, ce ferment du
vieux monde.*

    *Le nitre et le natron sont thèmes de l'exil. Nos
pensers courent à l'action sur des pistes osseuses.*

*L'éclair m'ouvre le lit de plus vastes desseins. L'orage
en vain déplace les bornes de l'absence.*

*Ceux-là qui furent se croiser aux grandes Indes
atlantiques, ceux-là qui flairent l'idée neuve aux
fraîcheurs de l'abîme, ceux-là qui soufflent dans les
cornes aux portes du futur*

*Savent qu'aux sables de l'exil sifflent les hautes
passions lovées sous le fouet de l'éclair . . . Ô Prodigue
sous le sel et l'écume de Juin! garde vivante parmi
nous la force occulte de ton chant!*

*Comme celui qui dit à l'émissaire, et c'est là
son message : « Voilez la face de nos femmes; levez
la face de nos fils; et la consigne est de laver la pierre
de vos seuils . . . Je vous dirai tout bas le nom des
sources où, demain, nous baignerons un pur cour-
roux. »*

*

Et c'est l'heure, ô Poète, de décliner ton nom,   15
ta naissance, et ta race . . .

PLUIES

A Katherine et Francis Biddle

I

   Le banyan de la pluie prend ses assises sur la
Ville,
   Un polypier hâtif monte à ses noces de corail
dans tout ce lait d'eau vive,
   Et l'Idée nue comme un rétiaire peigne aux
jardins du peuple sa crinière de fille.

   Chante, poème, à la criée des eaux l'imminence
du thème,
   Chante, poème, à la foulée des eaux l'évasion   5
du thème :
   Une haute licence aux flancs des Vierges
prophétiques,

   Une éclosion d'ovules d'or dans la nuit fauve
des vasières
   Et mon lit fait, ô fraude! à la lisière d'un tel
songe,
   Là où s'avive et croît et se prend à tourner la
rose obscène du poème.

   Seigneur terrible de mon rire, voici la terre   10
fumante au goût de venaison,
   L'argile veuve sous l'eau vierge, la terre lavée
du pas des hommes insomnieux,
   Et, flairée de plus près comme un vin, n'est-il
pas vrai qu'elle provoque la perte de mémoire?

   Seigneur, Seigneur terrible de mon rire! voici
l'envers du songe sur la terre,
   Comme la réponse des hautes dunes à l'étage-
ment des mers, voici, voici
   La terre à fin d'usage, l'heure nouvelle dans   15
ses langes, et mon cœur visité d'une étrange voyelle.

II

Nourrices très suspectes, Suivantes aux yeux voilés d'aînesse, ô Pluies par qui
L'homme insolite tient sa caste, que dirons-nous ce soir à qui prendra hauteur de notre veille?
Sur quelle couche nouvelle, à quelle tête rétive ravirons-nous encore l'étincelle qui vaille?

Muette l'Ande sur mon toit, j'ai une acclamation très forte en moi, et c'est pour vous, ô Pluies!
Je porterai ma cause devant vous: à la pointe de vos lances le plus clair de mon bien!   5
L'écume aux lèvres du poème comme un lait de coraux!

Et celle qui danse comme un psylle à l'entrée de mes phrases,
L'Idée, plus nue qu'un glaive au jeu des factions,
M'enseignera le rite et la mesure contre l'impatience du poème.

Seigneur terrible de mon rire, gardez-moi de   10
l'aveu, de l'accueil et du chant.
Seigneur terrible de mon rire, qu'il est d'offense aux lèvres de l'averse!
Qu'il est de fraudes consumées sous nos plus hautes migrations!

Dans la nuit claire de midi, nous avançons plus d'une proposition
Nouvelle, sur l'essence de l'être...Ô fumées que voilà sur la pierre de l'âtre!
Et la pluie tiède sur nos toits fit aussi bien   15
d'éteindre les lampes dans nos mains.

III

Sœurs des guerriers d'Assur furent les hautes Pluies en marche sur la terre :
Casquées de plume et haut-troussées, éperonnées d'argent et de cristal,
Comme Didon foulant l'ivoire aux portes de Carthage,

Comme l'épouse de Cortez, ivre d'argile et peinte, entre ses hautes plantes apocryphes . . .
Elles avivaient de nuit l'azur aux crosses de nos armes,   5
Elles peupleront l'Avril au fond des glaces de nos chambres !

Et je n'ai garde d'oublier leur piétinement au seuil des chambres d'ablution :
Guerrières, ô guerrières par la lance et le trait jusqu'à nous aiguisées !
Danseuses, ô danseuses par la danse et l'attrait au sol multipliées !

Ce sont des armes à brassées, ce sont des filles   10
par charretées, une distribution d'aigles aux légions,
Un soulèvement de piques aux faubourgs pour les plus jeunes peuples de la terre — faisceaux rompus de vierges dissolues,
Ô grandes gerbes non liées ! l'ample et vive moisson aux bras des hommes renversée !

. . . Et la Ville est de verre sur son socle d'ébène, la science aux bouches des fontaines,
Et l'étranger lit sur nos murs les grandes affiches annonaires,
Et la fraîcheur est dans nos murs, où l'In-   15
dienne ce soir logera chez l'habitant.

IV

Relations faites à l'Édile; confessions faites
à nos portes . . . Tue-moi, bonheur!
  Une langue nouvelle de toutes parts offerte!
une fraîcheur d'haleine par le monde
  Comme le souffle même de l'esprit, comme la
chose même proférée,

  A même l'être, son essence; à même la source,
sa naissance:
  Ha! toute l'affusion du dieu salubre sur nos   5
faces, et telle brise en fleur
  Au fil de l'herbe bleuissante, qui devance le
pas des plus lointaines dissidences!

  . . . Nourrices très suspectes, ô Semeuses de
spores, de semences et d'espèces légères,
  De quelles hauteurs déchues trahissez-vous pour
nous les voies,
  Comme au bas des orages les plus beaux êtres
lapidés sur la croix de leurs ailes?

  Que hantiez-vous si loin, qu'il faille encore   10
qu'on rêve à en perdre le vivre?
  Et de quelle autre condition nous parlez-vous
si bas qu'on en perde mémoire?
  Pour trafiquer de choses saintes parmi nous,
désertiez-vous vos couches, ô Simoniaques?

  Au frais commerce de l'embrun, là où le ciel
mûrit son goût d'arum et de névé,
  Vous fréquentiez l'éclair salace, et dans l'aubier
des grandes aubes lacérées,
  Au pur vélin rayé d'une amorce divine, vous   15
nous direz, ô Pluies! quelle langue nouvelle sollicitait
pour vous la grande onciale de feu vert.

V

Que votre approche fût pleine de grandeur, nous
le savions, hommes des villes, sur nos maigres scories,
Mais nous avions rêvé de plus hautaines confi-
dences au premier souffle de l'averse,
Et vous nous restituez, ô Pluies! à notre ins-
tance humaine, avec ce goût d'argile sous nos masques.

En de plus hauts parages chercherons-nous
mémoire? . . . ou s'il nous faut chanter l'oubli aux
bibles d'or des basses feuillaisons? . . .
Nos fièvres peintes aux tulipiers du songe, la   5
taie sur l'œil des pièces d'eau et la pierre roulée sur
la bouche des puits, voilà-t-il pas beaux thèmes à
reprendre,
Comme roses anciennes aux mains de l'inva-
lide de guerre? . . . La ruche encore est au verger,
l'enfance aux fourches du vieil arbre, et l'échelle
interdite aux beaux veuvages de l'éclair . . .

Douceur d'agave, d'aloès . . . fade saison de
l'homme sans méprise! C'est la terre lassée des
brûlures de l'esprit.
Les pluies vertes se peignent aux glaces des
banquiers. Aux linges tièdes des pleureuses s'effacera
la face des dieux-filles.
Et des idées nouvelles viennent en compte aux
bâtisseurs d'Empires sur leur table. Tout un peuple
muet se lève dans mes phrases, aux grandes marges
du poème.

Dressez, dressez, à bout de caps, les catafal-   10
ques du Habsbourg, les hauts bûchers de l'homme de
guerre, les hauts ruchers de l'imposture.

Vannez, vannez, à bout de caps, les grands ossuaires de l'autre guerre, les grands ossuaires de l'homme blanc sur qui l'enfance fut fondée.

Et qu'on évente sur sa chaise, sur sa chaise de fer, l'homme en proie aux visions dont s'irritent les peuples.

Nous n'en finirons pas de voir traîner sur l'étendue des mers la fumée des hauts faits où charbonne l'histoire,

Cependant qu'aux Chartreuses et aux Maladreries, un parfum de termites et de framboises blanches fait lever sur leurs claies les Princes grabataires :

« J'avais, j'avais ce goût de vivre chez les hommes, et voici que la terre exhale son âme d'étrangère ... »

15

VI

Un homme atteint de telle solitude, qu'il aille et qu'il suspende aux sanctuaires le masque et le bâton de commandement!
Moi je portais l'éponge et le fiel aux blessures d'un vieil arbre chargé des chaînes de la terre.
« J'avais, j'avais ce goût de vivre loin des hommes, et voici que les Pluies . . . »

Transfuges sans message, ô Mimes sans visage, vous meniez aux confins de si belles semailles!
Pour quels beaux feux d'herbages chez les hommes détournez-vous un soir vos pas, pour quelles histoires dénouées
Au feu des roses dans les chambres, dans les chambres où vit la sombre fleur du sexe?

5

Convoitiez-vous nos femmes et nos filles derrière la grille de leurs songes? (Il est des soins d'aînées
Au plus secret des chambres, il est de purs offices, et tels qu'on en rêverait aux palpes des insectes . . .)
N'avez-vous mieux à faire, chez nos fils, d'épier l'amer parfum viril aux buffleteries de guerre? (comme un peuple de Sphinges, lourdes du chiffre et de l'énigme, disputent du pouvoir aux portes des élus . . .)

Ô Pluies par qui les blés sauvages envahissent la Ville, et les chaussées de pierre se hérissent d'irascibles cactées,
Sous mille pas nouveaux sont mille pierres nouvelles fraîchement visitées . . . Aux éventaires rafraîchis d'une invisible plume, faites vos comptes, diamantaires!

10

Et l'homme dur entre les hommes, au milieu de la foule, se surprend à rêver de l'élyme des sables . . . « J'avais, j'avais ce goût de vivre sans douceur, et voici que les Pluies . . . » (La vie monte aux orages sur l'aile du refus.)

Passez, Métisses, et nous laissez à notre guet . . . Tel s'abreuve au divin dont le masque est d'argile.

Toute pierre lavée des signes de voirie, toute feuille lavée des signes de latrie, nous te lirons enfin, terre abluée des encres du copiste . . .

Passez, et nous laissez à nos plus vieux usages. Que ma parole encore aille devant moi! et nous chanterons encore un chant des hommes pour qui passe, un chant du large pour qui veille:

VII

« *Innombrables sont nos voies, et nos demeures*   1
incertaines. Tel s'abreuve au divin dont la lèvre est
d'argile. Vous, laveuses des morts dans les eaux-
mères du matin—et c'est la terre encore aux ronces
de la guerre — lavez aussi la face des vivants; lavez,
ô Pluies! la face triste des violents, la face douce des
violents . . . car leurs voies sont étroites, et leurs
demeures incertaines.

« *Lavez, ô Pluies! un lieu de pierre pour les*   2
forts. Aux grandes tables s'assiéront, sous l'auvent
de leur force, ceux que n'a point grisés le vin des
hommes, ceux que n'a point souillés le goût des
larmes ni du songe, ceux-là qui n'ont point cure de
leur nom dans les trompettes d'os . . . aux grandes
tables s'assiéront, sous l'auvent de leur force, en lieu
de pierre pour les forts.

« *Lavez le doute et la prudence au pas de*   3
l'action, lavez le doute et la décence au champ de la
vision. Lavez, ô Pluies! la taie sur l'œil de l'homme
de bien, sur l'œil de l'homme bien-pensant; lavez
la taie sur l'œil de l'homme de bon goût, sur l'œil de
l'homme de bon ton; la taie de l'homme de mérite,
la taie de l'homme de talent; lavez l'écaille sur l'œil
du Maître et du Mécène, sur l'œil du Juste et du
Notable . . . sur l'œil des hommes qualifiés pour la
prudence et la décence.

« *Lavez, lavez la bienveillance au cœur des*   4
grands Intercesseurs, la bienséance au front des
grands Éducateurs, et la souillure du langage sur
les lèvres publiques. Lavez, ô Pluies, la main du
Juge et du Prévôt, la main de l'accoucheuse et

de *l'ensevelisseuse, les mains léchées d'infirmes et
d'aveugles, et la main basse, au front des hommes,
qui rêve encore de rênes et du fouet . . . avec l'assenti-
ment des grands Intercesseurs, des grands Éduca-
teurs.*

« *Lavez, lavez l'histoire des peuples aux*   5
*hautes tables de mémoire: les grandes annales
officielles, les grandes chroniques du Clergé et les
bulletins académiques. Lavez les bulles et les chartes,
et les Cahiers du Tiers-État; les Covenants, les
Pactes d'alliance et les grands actes fédératifs;
lavez, lavez, ô Pluies! tous les vélins et tous les
parchemins, couleur de murs d'asiles et de léproseries,
couleur d'ivoire fossile et de vieilles dents de mules . . .
Lavez, lavez, ô Pluies! les hautes tables de mémoire.*

« *Ô Pluies! lavez au cœur de l'homme les*   6
*plus beaux dits de l'homme: les plus belles sentences,
les plus belles séquences; les phrases les mieux faites,
les pages les mieux nées. Lavez, lavez, au cœur des
hommes, leur goût de cantilènes, d'élégies; leur goût
de villanelles et de rondeaux; leurs grands bonheurs
d'expression; lavez le sel de l'atticisme et le miel
de l'euphuisme, lavez, lavez la literie du songe et la
litière du savoir: au cœur de l'homme sans refus,
au cœur de l'homme sans dégoût, lavez, lavez, ô
Pluies! les plus beaux dons de l'homme . . . au cœur
des hommes les mieux doués pour les grandes œuvres
de raison. »*

VIII

. . . Le banyan de la pluie perd ses assises sur
la Ville. Au vent du ciel la chose errante et telle
        Qu'elle s'en vint vivre parmi nous! . . . Et vous
ne nierez pas, soudain, que tout nous vienne à rien.
        Qui veut savoir ce qu'il advient des pluies en
marche sur la terre, s'en vienne vivre sur mon toit,
parmi les signes et présages.

        Promesses non tenues! Inlassables semailles!
Et fumées que voilà sur la chaussée des hommes!
        Vienne l'éclair, ha! qui nous quitte! . . . Et   5
nous reconduirons aux portes de la Ville
        Les hautes Pluies en marche sous l'Avril, les
hautes Pluies en marche sous le fouet comme un
Ordre de Flagellants.

        Mais nous voici livrés plus nus à ce parfum
d'humus et de benjoin où s'éveille la terre au goût
de vierge noire.
        . . . C'est la terre plus fraîche au cœur des fou-
geraies, l'affleurement des grands fossiles aux marnes
ruisselantes,
        Et dans la chair navrée des roses après l'orage,
la terre, la terre encore au goût de femme faite femme.

        C'est la Ville plus vive aux feux de mille
glaives, le vol des sacres sur les marbres, le ciel
encore aux vasques des fontaines,
        Et la truie d'or à bout de stèle sur les places
désertes. C'est la splendeur encore aux porches de
cinabre; la bête noire ferrée d'argent à la plus basse
porte des jardins;
        C'est le désir encore au flanc des jeunes veuves,   10
des jeunes veuves de guerriers, comme de grandes
urnes rescellées.

...C'est la fraîcheur courant aux crêtes du langage, l'écume encore aux lèvres du poème,

Et l'homme encore de toutes parts pressé d'idées nouvelles, qui cède au soulèvement des grandes houles de l'esprit :

« Le beau chant, le beau chant que voilà sur la dissipation des eaux !... » et mon poème, ô Pluies ! qui ne fut pas écrit !

IX

La nuit venue, les grilles closes, que pèse l'eau du ciel au bas-empire des taillis ?

A la pointe des lances le plus clair de mon bien !... Et toutes choses égales, au fléau de l'esprit,

Seigneur terrible de mon rire, vous porterez ce soir l'esclandre en plus haut lieu.

*

...Car telles sont vos délices, Seigneur, au seuil aride du poème, où mon rire épouvante les paons verts de la gloire.

NEIGES

A Françoise-Renée Saint-Léger Léger

I

Et puis vinrent les neiges, les premières neiges   1
de l'absence, sur les grands lés tissés du songe et du
réel ; et toute peine remise aux hommes de mémoire,
il y eut une fraîcheur de linges à nos tempes. Et ce
fut au matin, sous le sel gris de l'aube, un peu avant
la sixième heure, comme en un havre de fortune, un
lieu de grâce et de merci où licencier l'essaim des
grandes odes du silence.

Et toute la nuit, à notre insu, sous ce haut fait   2
de plume, portant très haut vestige et charge d'âmes,
les hautes villes de pierre ponce forées d'insectes
lumineux n'avaient cessé de croître et d'exceller, dans
l'oubli de leur poids. Et ceux-là seuls en surent
quelque chose, dont la mémoire est incertaine et le
récit est aberrant. La part que prit l'esprit à ces
choses insignes, nous l'ignorons.

Nul n'a surpris, nul n'a connu, au plus haut   3
front de pierre, le premier affleurement de cette heure
soyeuse, le premier attouchement de cette chose fragile
et très futile, comme un frôlement de cils. Sur les
revêtements de bronze et sur les élancements d'acier
chromé, sur les moellons de sourde porcelaine et sur
les tuiles de gros verre, sur la fusée de marbre noir et sur
l'éperon de métal blanc, nul n'a surpris, nul n'a terni

cette buée d'un souffle à sa naissance, comme   4
la première transe d'une lame mise à nu ... Il neigeait,
et voici, nous en dirons merveilles: l'aube muette
dans sa plume, comme une grande chouette fabuleuse en
proie aux souffles de l'esprit, enflait son corps de dahlia
blanc. Et de tous les côtés il nous était prodige et fête.
Et le salut soit sur la face des terrasses, où l'Architecte,
l'autre été, nous a montré des œufs d'engoulevent !

II

*Je sais que des vaisseaux en peine dans tout
ce naissain pâle poussent leur meuglement de bêtes
sourdes contre la cécité des hommes et des dieux;
et toute la misère du monde appelle le pilote au large
des estuaires. Je sais qu'aux chutes des grands fleuves
se nouent d'étranges alliances, entre le ciel et l'eau:
de blanches noces de noctuelles, de blanches fêtes de
phryganes. Et sur les vastes gares enfumées d'aube
comme des palmeraies sous verre, la nuit laiteuse
engendre une fête du gui.*

*Et il y a aussi cette sirène des usines, un peu
avant la sixième heure et la relève du matin, dans ce
pays, là-haut, de très grands lacs, où les chantiers
illuminés toute la nuit tendent sur l'espalier du ciel
une haute treille sidérale: mille lampes choyées des
choses grèges de la neige ... De grandes nacres en
croissance, de grandes nacres sans défaut médi-
tent-elles leur réponse au plus profond des eaux?
—ô toutes choses à renaître, ô vous toute réponse!
Et la vision enfin sans faille et sans défaut! ...*

*Il neige sur les dieux de fonte et sur les aciéries
cinglées de brèves liturgies; sur le mâchefer et sur
l'ordure et sur l'herbage des remblais: il neige sur
la fièvre et sur l'outil des hommes — neige plus fine
qu'au désert la graine de coriandre, neige plus fraîche
qu'en avril le premier lait des jeunes bêtes ... Il neige
par là-bas vers l'Ouest, sur les silos et sur les ranchs
et sur les vastes plaines sans histoire enjambées de
pylônes; sur les tracés de villes à naître et sur la
cendre morte des camps levés;*

sur les hautes terres non rompues, envenimées

2

*d'acides, et sur les hordes d'abiès noirs empêtrés
d'aigles barbelés, comme des trophées de guerre...
Que disiez-vous, trappeur, de vos deux mains congé-
diées? Et sur la hache du pionnier quelle inquiétante
douceur a cette nuit posé la joue?... Il neige, hors
chrétienté, sur les plus jeunes ronces et sur les bêtes
les plus neuves. Épouse du monde ma présence!...
Et quelque part au monde où le silence éclaire un songe
de mélèze, la tristesse soulève son masque de servante.*

III

Ce n'était pas assez que tant de mers, ce n'était 1
pas assez que tant de terres eussent dispersé la course
de nos ans. Sur la rive nouvelle où nous halons,
charge croissante, le filet de nos routes, encore fal-
lait-il tout ce plain-chant des neiges pour nous ravir
la trace de nos pas... Par les chemins de la plus vaste
terre étendrez-vous le sens et la mesure de nos ans,
neiges prodigues de l'absence, neiges cruelles au
cœur des femmes où s'épuise l'attente?

Et Celle à qui je pense entre toutes femmes de 2
ma race, du fond de son grand âge lève à son Dieu
sa face de douceur. Et c'est un pur lignage qui tient
sa grâce en moi. « Qu'on nous laisse tous deux à ce
langage sans paroles dont vous avez l'usage, ô vous
toute présence, ô vous toute patience! Et comme un
grand Ave de grâce sur nos pas chante tout bas le
chant très pur de notre race. Et il y a un si long temps
que veille en moi cette affre de douceur...

Dame de haut parage fut votre âme muette à 3
l'ombre de vos croix; mais chair de pauvre femme,
en son grand âge, fut votre cœur vivant de femme en
toutes femmes suppliciée... Au cœur du beau pays
captif où nous brûlerons l'épine, c'est bien grande
pitié des femmes de tout âge à qui le bras des hommes
fit défaut. Et qui donc vous mènera, dans ce plus
grand veuvage, à vos Églises souterraines où la
lampe est frugale, et l'abeille, divine?

...Et tout ce temps de mon silence en terre 4
lointaine, aux roses pâles des ronciers j'ai vu pâlir
l'usure de vos yeux. Et vous seule aviez grâce de ce
mutisme au cœur de l'homme comme une pierre

noire ... Car nos années sont terres de mouvance dont
nul ne tient le fief, mais comme un grand Ave de
grâce sur nos pas nous suit au loin le chant de pur
lignage; et il y a un si long temps que veille en nous
cette affre de douceur ...

     Neigeait-il, cette nuit, de ce côté du monde où   5
vous joignez les mains? ... Ici, c'est bien grand bruit
de chaînes par les rues, où vont courant les hommes
à leur ombre. Et l'on ne savait pas qu'il y eût encore
au monde tant de chaînes, pour équiper les roues en
fuite vers le jour. Et c'est aussi grand bruit de pelles
à nos portes, ô vigiles! Les nègres de voirie vont
sur les aphtes de la terre comme gens de gabelle. Une
lampe

     survit au cancer de la nuit. Et un oiseau de   6
cendre rose, qui fut de braise tout l'été, illumine sou-
dain les cryptes de l'hiver, comme l'Oiseau du Phase
aux Livres d'heures de l'An Mille ... Épouse du
monde ma présence, épouse du monde mon attente!
Que nous ravisse encore la fraîche haleine de men-
songe! ... Et la tristesse des hommes est dans les
hommes, mais cette force aussi qui n'a de nom, et
cette grâce, par instants, dont il faut bien qu'ils
aient souri. »

IV

    Seul à faire le compte, du haut de cette chambre   1
d'angle qu'environne un Océan de neiges.—Hôte
précaire de l'instant, homme sans preuve ni témoin,
détacherai-je mon lit bas comme une pirogue de sa
crique? . . . Ceux qui campent chaque jour plus loin
du lieu de leur naissance, ceux qui tirent chaque jour
leur barque sur d'autres rives, savent mieux chaque
jour le cours des choses illisibles; et remontant les
fleuves vers leur source, entre les vertes apparences,
ils sont gagnés soudain de cet éclat sévère où toute
langue perd ses armes.

    Ainsi l'homme mi-nu sur l'Océan des neiges,   2
rompant soudain l'immense libration, poursuit un
singulier dessein où les mots n'ont plus prise. Épouse
du monde ma présence, épouse du monde ma pru-
dence! . . . Et du côté des eaux premières me retournant
avec le jour, comme le voyageur, à la néoménie, dont
la conduite est incertaine et la démarche est aberrante,
voici que j'ai dessein d'errer parmi les plus vieilles
couches du langage, parmi les plus hautes tranches
phonétiques: jusqu'à des langues très lointaines,
jusqu'à des langues très entières et très parcimo-
nieuses,

    comme ces langues dravidiennes qui n'eurent   3
pas de mots distincts pour « hier » et pour « demain ».
Venez et nous suivez, qui n'avons mots à dire: nous
remontons ce pur délice sans graphie où court
l'antique phrase humaine; nous nous mouvons parmi
de claires élisions, des résidus d'anciens préfixes
ayant perdu leur initiale, et devançant les beaux
travaux de linguistique, nous nous frayons nos voies
nouvelles jusqu'à ces locutions inouïes, où l'aspira-

tion recule au-delà des voyelles et la modulation du
souffle se propage, au gré de telles labiales mi-sonores,
en quête de pures finales vocaliques.

    ... Et ce fut au matin, sous le plus pur vocable,   4
un beau pays sans haine ni lésine, un lieu de grâce
et de merci pour la montée des sûrs présages de
l'esprit; et comme un grand Ave *de grâce sur nos*
pas, la grande roseraie blanche de toutes neiges à
la ronde ... Fraîcheur d'ombelles, de corymbes, fraî-
cheur d'arille sous la fève, ha! tant d'azyme encore
aux lèvres de l'errant! ... Quelle flore nouvelle, en
lieu plus libre, nous absout de la fleur et du fruit?
Quelle navette d'os aux mains des femmes de grand
âge, quelle amande d'ivoire aux mains des femmes
de jeune âge

    nous tissera linge plus frais pour la brûlure   5
des vivants? ... Épouse du monde notre patience,
épouse du monde notre attente! ... Ah! tout l'hièble
du songe à même notre visage! Et nous ravisse encore,
ô monde! ta fraîche haleine de mensonge! ... Là où
les fleuves encore sont guéables, là où les neiges encore
sont guéables, nous passerons ce soir une âme non
guéable ... Et au-delà sont les grands lés du songe,
et tout ce bien fongible où l'être engage sa fortune ...

*

    Désormais cette page où plus rien ne s'inscrit.   6

POEME A L'ETRANGERE

"Alien Registration Act".

I

Les sables ni les chaumes n'enchanteront le pas des siècles à venir, où fut la rue pour vous pavée d'une pierre sans mémoire — ô pierre inexorable et verte plus que n'est
le sang vert des Castilles à votre tempe d'Étrangère !

Une éternité de beau temps pèse aux membranes closes du silence, et la maison de bois qui bouge, à fond d'abîme, sur ses ancres, mûrit un fruit de lampes à midi
pour de plus tièdes couvaisons de souffrances nouvelles.

Mais les tramways à bout d'usure qui s'en furent un soir au tournant de la rue, qui s'en furent sur rails au pays des Atlantes, par les chaussées et par les rampes
et les ronds-points d'Observatoires envahis de sargasses,

par les quartiers d'eaux vives et de Zoos hantés des gens de cirques, par les quartiers de Nègres et d'Asiates aux migrations d'alevins, et par les beaux solstices verts des places rondes comme des attolls,
(là où campait un soir la cavalerie des Fédéraux, ô mille têtes d'hippocampes !)

chantant l'hier, chantant l'ailleurs, chantaient le mal à sa naissance, et, sur deux notes d'Oiseau-chat, l'Été boisé des jeunes Capitales infestées de cigales . . . Or voici bien, à votre porte, laissés pour compte à l'Étrangère,

5

ces deux rails, ces deux rails — d'où venus? —
qui n'ont pas dit leur dernier mot.

*

« Rue Gît-le-cœur . . . Rue Gît-le-cœur . . . » chante
tout bas l'Alienne sous ses lampes, et ce sont là
méprises de sa langue d'Étrangère.

II

« . . . *Non point des larmes—l'aviez-vous cru?*
— mais ce mal de la vue qui nous vient, à la longue,
d'une trop grande fixité du glaive sur toutes braises
de ce monde,
            (ô sabre de Strogoff à hauteur de nos cils!)

            peut-être aussi l'épine, sous la chair, d'une
plus jeune ronce au cœur des femmes de ma race; et
j'en conviens aussi, l'abus de ces trop longs cigares de
veuve jusqu'à l'aube, parmi le peuple de mes lampes,
            dans tout ce bruit de grandes eaux que fait la
nuit du Nouveau Monde.

            . . . Vous qui chantez — c'est votre chant —   5
vous qui chantez tous bannissements au monde, ne
me chanterez-vous pas un chant du soir à la mesure
de mon mal? un chant de grâce pour mes lampes,
            un chant de grâce pour l'attente, et pour l'aube
plus noire au cœur des althæas?

            De la violence sur la terre il nous est fait si
large mesure . . . Ô vous, homme de France, ne ferez-
vous pas encore que j'entende, sous l'humaine saison,
parmi les cris de martinets et toutes cloches ursulines,
monter dans l'or des pailles et dans la poudre de vos
Rois
            un rire de lavandières aux ruelles de pierre?

            . . . Ne dites pas qu'un oiseau chante, et qu'il
est, sur mon toit, vêtu de très beau rouge comme
Prince d'Église. Ne dites pas — vous l'avez vu —
que l'écureuil est sur la véranda; et l'enfant-aux-
journaux, les Sœurs quêteuses et le laitier. Ne dites
pas qu'à fond de ciel

*un couple d'aigles, depuis hier, tient la Ville
sous le charme de ses grandes manières.*

*Car tout cela est-il bien vrai, qui n'a d'histoire
ni de sens, qui n'a de trêve ni mesure?... Oui tout
cela qui n'est pas clair, et ne m'est rien, et pèse moins
qu'à mes mains nues de femme une clé d'Europe
teinte de sang... Ah! tout cela est-il bien vrai?...
(et qu'est-ce encore, sur mon seuil,*

*que cet oiseau vert-bronze, d'allure peu catho-
lique, qu'ils appellent Starling?) »*

*

*« Rue Gît-le-cœur... Rue Gît-le-cœur... » chan-
tent tout bas les cloches en exil, et ce sont là méprises
de leur langue d'étrangères.*

III

Dieux proches, dieux sanglants, faces peintes
et closes! Sous l'orangerie des lampes à midi mûrit
l'abîme le plus vaste. Et cependant que le flot monte
à vos persiennes closes, l'Été déjà sur son déclin,
virant la chaîne de ses ancres,
  vire aux grandes roses d'équinoxe comme aux
verrières des Absides.

  Et c'est déjà le troisième an que le fruit du
mûrier fait aux chaussées de votre rue de si belles
taches de vin mûr, comme on en voit au cœur des
althæas, comme on en vit aux seins des filles d'Éloa.
Et c'est déjà le troisième an qu'à votre porte close,
  comme un nid de Sibylles, l'abîme enfante ses
merveilles: lucioles!

  Dans l'Été vert comme une impasse, dans l'Été   5
vert de si beau vert, quelle aube tierce, ivre créance,
ouvre son aile de locuste? Bientôt les hautes brises
de Septembre tiendront conseil aux portes de la Ville,
sur les savanes d'aviation, et dans un grand avène-
ment d'eaux libres
  la Ville encore au fleuve versera toute sa récolte
de cigales mortes d'un Été.

  . . . Et toujours il y a ce grand éclat du verre,
et tout ce haut suspens. Et toujours il y a ce bruit de
grandes eaux. Et parfois c'est Dimanche, et par les
tuyauteries des chambres, montant des fosses atlan-
tides, avec ce goût de l'incréé comme une haleine
d'outre-monde,
  c'est un parfum d'abîme et de néant parmi les
moisissures de la terre . . .

Poème à l'Étrangère! Poème à l'Émigrée!...
Chaussée de crêpe ou d'amarante entre vos hautes
malles inécloses! Ô grande par le cœur et par le cri
de votre race!... L'Europe saigne à vos flancs comme
la Vierge du Toril. Vos souliers de bois d'or furent
aux vitrines de l'Europe
     et les sept glaives de vermeil de Votre Dame   10
des Angoisses.

     Les cavaleries encore sont aux églises de vos
pères, humant l'astre de bronze aux grilles des autels.
Et les hautes lances de Bréda montent la garde au
pas des portes de famille. Mais plus d'un cœur bien
né s'en fut à la canaille. Et il y avait aussi bien à
redire à cette enseigne du bonheur, sur vos golfes
trop bleus,
     comme le palmier d'or au fond des boîtes à
cigares.

     Dieux proches, dieux fréquents! quelle rose
de fer nous forgerez-vous demain? L'Oiseau-moqueur
est sur nos pas! Et cette histoire n'est pas nouvelle
que le Vieux Monde essaime à tous les siècles, comme
un rouge pollen... Sur le tambour voilé des lampes
à midi, nous mènerons encore plus d'un deuil, chan-
tant l'hier, chantant l'ailleurs, chantant le mal à sa
naissance
     et la splendeur de vivre qui s'exile à perte
d'hommes cette année.

     Mais ce soir de grand âge et de grande patience,   15
dans l'Été lourd d'opiats et d'obscures laitances,
pour délivrer à fond d'abîme le peuple de vos lampes,
ayant, homme très seul, pris par ce haut quartier de
Fondations d'aveugles, de Réservoirs mis au linceul
et de vallons en cage pour les morts, longeant les grilles
et les lawns et tous ces beaux jardins à l'italienne
     dont les maîtres un soir s'en furent épouvantés
d'un parfum de sépulcre,

*je m'en vais, ô mémoire! à mon pas d'homme
libre, sans horde ni tribu, parmi le chant des sabliers,
et, le front nu, lauré d'abeilles de phosphore, au bas
du ciel très vaste d'acier vert comme en un fond de
mer, sifflant mon peuple de Sibylles, sifflant mon
peuple d'incrédules, je flatte encore en songe, de la
main, parmi tant d'êtres invisibles,*

*ma chienne d'Europe qui fut blanche et, plus
que moi, poète.*

*

*« Rue Gît-le-cœur . . . Rue Gît-le-cœur . . . » chante
tout bas l'Ange à Tobie, et ce sont là méprises de sa
langue d'Étranger.*

NOTES

PREFACE

1. See e.g. S. W. Taylor and E. Lucie-Smith (eds.), *French Poetry Today*, Rapp & Whiting/Deutsch, 1971, p. 403. The writers' view of Perse as a surrealist (p. 23) does, of course, undermine one's confidence in their judgement.

INTRODUCTION

2. The abbreviated reference 'Pléiade' is to the Saint-John Perse volume in the Bibliothèque de la Pléiade, Gallimard, 1972.

3. Quoted by Michel Soulié, *La Vie politique d'Edouard Herriot*, Colin, 1962, p. 493. An abbreviated version is given in *Honneur à Saint-John Perse*, Gallimard, 1965, p. 713. This important volume is referred to simply as '*Honneur*'.

4. E.g. Claudel, 'Paroles au Maréchal' which the poet later recanted, calling the ode 'un monument élevé à la fois à la Naïveté et à l'Imposture' (*Œuvre poétique*, Gallimard, Bibliothèque de la Pléiade, 1962, p. 586); Gide, *Journal*, 9–19 July 1940; Valéry, who had pronounced the speech of thanks on Pétain's admission to the Académie française in 1931, was no less delighted at 'order' triumphing over 'chaos'.

5. Elizabeth R. Cameron, 'Alexis Saint-Léger Léger' in *The Diplomats, 1919–1939*, Princeton University Press, 1953, p. 404.

6. Katherine Biddle, letter to R.L., Washington D.C., 6 June 1970; see also note to 'Exil', 1, 1, below.

7. See monograph, pp. 27-8.

8. See monograph, pp. 103. ff for a general presentation of the dialectic of exile.

9. Mallarmé, *Œuvres complètes*, Gallimard (Bibliothèque de la Pléiade), 1956, p. 503.

10. Otten suggests that the first canto 'se passe au matin, au lever du soleil', but this does not seem to tally with the suggested heat of the sun. Perse indeed recalls a 'coucher de soleil' (Pléiade, p. 576).

11. Gilbert Durand, 'Psychanalyse de la neige', *Mercure de France*, August 1953, 624.

12. For a fuller treatment of this aspect, see my 'Language as Imagery

in Saint-John Perse', *Forum for Modern Language Studies*, vi, 2, April 1970, 127–39.

13. Arthur J. Knodel, 'The Imagery of Saint-John Perse's "Neiges" ', *PMLA*, lxx, i, March 1955, 10; the article is translated in *Honneur*, pp. 447–60.

14. Durand, art. cit., p. 619.

15. Cf. Nerval's sense of failure in this respect expressed in his own pessimistic 'Epitaphe': 'Il voulait tout savoir mais il n'a rien connu'.

16. Claudel, *Œuvres en prose*, Gallimard, Bibliothèque de la Pléiade, 1965, p. 1247.

N.B. Only three words (*azalaïe, guifette* and *abiès*) in the four poems of *Exil* do not figure in *Le Nouveau Petit Larousse illustré*. The reader is therefore referred to this *vademecum* of all French students for any word not explained in the notes which may nonetheless be unfamiliar to him.

'EXIL'

Dedication: Archibald MacLeish (1892–), American poet and public servant, admired Perse's work from his period in Paris (1923–8) although he did not then make Leger's acquaintance. When Perse was exiled and settled in Washington, MacLeish was instrumental, as Librarian of Congress, in obtaining a private bursary for him to work as literary adviser. He is the author of a number of articles on Perse and his work which were important in presenting Perse to the American public. The letter sent to him with the manuscript of 'Exil' is brief but interesting:

9 Sept. 1941

Mon cher Archie,
Voici mon poème sur l'exil. Il est à vous. Disposez-en comme vous voudrez. Il m'aura permis du moins un geste de confiance envers un poète que j'admire, envers un homme que j'aime.

Si vous pouvez le faire dactylographier, vous m'en donnerez les exemplaires à réviser: j'en garderai quelques-uns, car je n'ai pour moi-même qu'un mauvais brouillon; et je dois aussi à notre amie Katherine [Biddle] de lui communiquer, avant impression, ce poème écrit chez elle.

Je ne sais d'ailleurs si une telle œuvre peut être publiée aux Etats-Unis en français. Et elle serait intraduisible: non pas tant intellectuellement, dans ses abstractions, ses ellipses et ses "ambiguïtés" voulues, que physiquement, dans ses allitérations, ses assonances et ses incantations (astreintes au rythme de la vague)— Littéralement

4—E * *

aussi, dans les ressources étymologiques de certains de ses mots, les plus immatériels et les plus simples.

Parmi ses mots concrets, un seul mot rare ou exotique, dont je m'excuse: "azalaïe", que vous ne trouveriez pas dans les dictionnaires usuels, est le nom de la grande caravane annuelle du sel aux déserts d'Afrique. J'en avais besoin pour une transposition.

Affectueusement

A.L.

I

1. Note the parallel phrasing and Latinate construction of opening: ablative absolute followed (1, 2) by dative of possession. The Roman tradition was to close the gates of the Temple of Janus, god of the threshold, in time of peace and open them in time of war (cf. note to VII, 12). Mrs Biddle recalls: 'Climbing the high dune where our "maison de verre" was perched, he stood once more facing the sea—as he wrote me "cette mer qui n'est jamais l'exil, étant tout l'exil." ' (K. G. Chapin, 'Poet of Wide Horizons', *The Quarterly Journal of the Library of Congress*, XXVII, 2, April 1970, 106.)

2. *clés.* Those of the beach-house, but also those of exile: cf. V, 6 below. *phare.* The old red brick Barnegat lighthouse on Long Beach Island, N.J. Although not directly visible from the beach-house its light could be seen at night.

l'astre roué vif. There was some controversy as to the reference here, ranging from an interpretation of the image as a swastika, Hitler's emblem thus being evoked at the outset of what is seen as a Resistance poem (Maurice Saillet, p. 84) to seeing it as nothing but the sun's bright reflection (Albert Henry: 'l'uomo contempla sulla soglia la luce di una estate bianca che schizza sulla pietra come se il sole stesso vi fosse arruotato vivo', 'Storia e critica interna', *Strumenti critici*, II, 5, February 1968, p. 84). Monique Parent sees first the sun's reflection and then the symbol of France's glory—and that of the poet—ruined by war (*Saint-John Perse et quelques devanciers*, p. 216). Perse stated quite specifically to Pierre Mazars that ' "Exil" n'est pas une image de la Résistance' (Pléiade, p. 576) and reacted strongly against Saillet's interpretation: 'Un plus libre réflexe, affranchi d'associations d'idées, lui eût épargné l'invraisemblable tentation de voir: une swastika, dans un vulgaire coucher de soleil sur une grève déserte; [and, referring to 1, 3] une délégation morale à l'emigration politique, dans le simple dépôt matériel d'une clé au voisinage d'une maison isolée . . .' (Pléiade, p. 553). An interesting syntactical point is the colon at the end of the line, suggesting that it is 'l'astre roué vif' which is speaking the following lines. It thus becomes a metaphor of the poet who seems to connect himself with Prometheus, whose theft of fire from heaven (from the sun in some accounts) is symbolised in lightning (see I, 7). The image of the swastika, far from being restricted to Hitler's Germany, is an ancient sun-symbol based on the cross with its arms crooked to indicate rotatory movement. The light of the sun itself seems tortured (racked on the wheel) to correspond at a cosmic level with the poet's sufferings: the poem is not an intimate cry of private despair but an expression of the universal plight of man in exile.

la pierre du seuil. Note how the poem opens and closes (VII, 14) on the threshold. The importance of this motif is considered both in the introduction, pp. 20 ff. and in the monograph, pp. 109–10.

3. *Mon hôte.* Francis Biddle, then U.S. Attorney General, and his wife Katherine. Note the desire to be alone (cf. I, 5).

maison de verre. The beach-house, 'Harvey Cedars', belonging to the Biddles. Perse later wrote to Katherine Biddle: 'Si vous dormez où j'ai dormi, dans cette chambre du haut face à l'Atlantique, sachez que je n'y ai jamais ouvert les yeux à l'aube, ni vu le soleil s'encastrer dans ma fenêtre, sans une pensée émue pour tout ce que je vous devais, à Francis et à vous. Depuis que je suis entré dans mon épreuve de proscrit je n'ai jamais respiré un peu librement, loin des miens, qu'auprès de vous deux et sous votre toit' (Pléiade, p. 903). And again: 'Je pense encore à Harvey Cedars, à ce dernier été consumé, entre nous, dans la maison de verre aux boiseries odorantes . . .' (p. 908).

4. *L'Eté de gypse aiguise ses fers de lance.* A superb transferred epithet. 'Gypse fer de lance' is a natural macle of gypsum formed by two rhomboid crystals being joined to give the arrowhead shape. Unlike the more familiar treated forms such as alabaster, it is yellowish rather than white in colour and shiny rather than matt, and it is crystalline, not powdery. Its appropriateness as an epithet for summer is all the greater. For another transferred epithet connected with gypsum, see IV, 15.

5. *flagrant.* Note proximity to Latin *flagrans.*

l'ossuaire des saisons. (see notes II, 12; VI, 4f). *saisons* = 'life' or 'passing years', cf. for Perse's choice and for the connection with intellectual activity VI, 3b: 'un lieu de cinéraires pour la délectation du sage.'

6. *Et, sur toutes grèves de ce monde.* The first instance of the refrain phrase emphasising the universality of his theme.

l'esprit du dieu fumant. Another image open to various interpretations deriving from the visual effect of the heat-haze rising from the beach. Knodel sees in it 'the violence that was loosed on the world at that moment' (p. 63). It may also be linked with inspiration (cf. *Vents* II, 6: 'O Poète . . . homme assailli du dieu!') and connected with the power of the sun (Phoebus Apollo, god of sun and poetry).

amiante. The non-inflammable substance suggests that the process continues indefinitely. Behind the immediate sense of 'asbestos', note the Greek etymon ἀμίαντος 'pure'.

7. *spasmes de l'éclair'* Note the sexual overtone (cf. 'l'éclair salace', 'Pluies' IV, 14). Silent discharges of summer lightning.

ravissement. The abstract sense is to the fore.

Princes en Tauride. In Euripides' *Iphigenia,* Orestes faces the Furies on a lonely beach in exile in Tauris.

II

2. *D'autres saisissent . . . la corne peinte des autels.* An action taken within the confines of four orthodox walls is contrasted with the poet's own position, staking everything on the 'lieu flagrant et nul' of the beach. The ancient Romans seized the horns of the altar to swear undying loyalty; in the Bible, on the two occasions when the horns are grasped, the motivation is fear (I Kings i, 50–1 and ii, 28). The former meaning is uppermost here.

3. *Pérégrin.* A foreigner living in ancient Rome (*peregrinus* > *pèlerin*), here equated with the poet as a foreign traveller.

4. *syrtes.* Originally areas of quicksands (Syrtis major, S. minor) off the North African coast, here generalised as shifting sands of 'l'aire la plus nue' (cf. I, 5). One might have suspected an echo of a line from Virgil ('Hunc ego Gaetulis agerem si *Syrtibus exsul . . .*', *Aeneid,* v, 51) were it not that Perse's antipathy for the *Aeneid* would lead one rather to suppose that he is using the words at their face value to express the sense of exile as uncertainty and treachery par excellence.

5. *frondes.* Both 'fronds' and 'slings', though the latter is uppermost. Slings and conches produce only a single note, an appropriately stark accompaniment to the exile's poem.

6. *vaisseaux creux.* It seems highly improbable that this should be taken in the sense of 'ships' despite the use of the epithet by Homer and Virgil (e.g. 'vela damus vastumque *cava trabe* currimus aequor', *Aeneid,* III, 191). Perse would never consider a ship among 'lieux vains et fades'.

6–7. Note the precariousness and emptiness of chosen settling-places. (cf. Book of Job xx, xxi).

8. The use of quotation marks indicates that the poet is not here speaking in his own voice. The speaker here is all-knowing and all-seeing in both time and space. An interior dialogue is engaged between the discriminating poet and the more indiscriminate inspiration within him (cf. a similar dialogue between Claudel and 'la Muse qui est la Grâce'). See note to III, 1.

la famille des Jules. The *gens Julia* of which Julius Caesar was a member.

Implied in the opening 'points de suspension' is the suggestion that the poet is enjoying more direct inspiration than either the *gens Julia* (of priestly caste supposedly descended from Venus) or actual sacerdotal mediators between the worshippers and divine inspiration.

9. *Où vont les sables à leur chant*. The sound of wind relentlessly shifting sands (cf. *Amers*, Strophe, IX, 3–2: 'la migration des sables vers la mer'), particularly towards the sea (cf. I, 14). The image is symbolic of the material being surpassed.

Princes de l'exil. Cf. VI, 8.

10. *furent*. 'went' (cf. IV, 10) (continuing 'vont', II, 9, but allowing the shift to 'furent' = 'were', II, 11). Notice the abrupt changes of tense in this *laisse*.

soyeuse. For this fragile silken quality, cf. 'Neiges' I, 3.

luthier. Maker of stringed instruments in general.

11. *mâchoire d'âne*. Cf. Judges xv, 15–17.

12. The alliteration powerfully supports the sense; cf. 'l'ossuaire des saisons' (I, 5). A beach on the north island of Guadeloupe is known as the 'Plage des ossements' or 'Plage des crânes' because of the bones periodically washed ashore, the relics of battles between the natives, the French and the English. The widespread connection between stones and bones (rocks being the 'bones' of Mother Earth) means we need not restrict the idea to such a reference, however.

14. *Les milices du vent*. On the ambiguous driving force of the wind, see monograph (on *Vents*), pp. 27–40.

15. *Sagesse de l'écume*. Recognition that 'omnia vanitas' (cf. IV, 16); but note too the important 'écume aux lèvres du poème' in 'Pluies', II, 6 and VIII, 13.

pestilences. The meaning is broader than in modern French.

la crépitation du sel. Designates the sea breaking on the shore. But Michel Otten (in his unpublished study of the poem, Louvain Univ., 1959–60) offers an extra, ingenious, reference: 'Pour obtenir un sel pur, on place les minerais dans d'immenses chaudières en tôle et, pour faciliter l'opération, les eaux sont additionnées de *chaux* (= le chaulage). On fait bouillir et, par suite du départ de l'eau, les cristaux de sel *crépitent*. Le verset serait donc une description technique très précise de cette purification du sel.' This seems inappropriately technical, but there is a process of decantation of the suffering suggested by this line and the next.

le lait de chaux vive. 'Lait de chaux' and 'chaux vive' are one and the same thing. Perse wants to underline the whiteness of the foaming waves and emphasise the importance of an almost ritual purification in the creative process. In certain creation myths the sea is churned into a milky life-producing substance (e.g. in the *Ramayana*).

18. *cirque*. Here obviously in Latin sense of 'sky'.

l'élancement des signes les plus fastes. Celestial signs used for augury; cf. 'signes du zodiaque'.

21. *Étranger.* The archetypal characterisation of the uprooted poet: the constant immediacy of exile is underlined. Past ('vestiges') and future ('prémisses') are unreal and unknown in the heightened awareness of the present, in which everything, even the sources of the poem he is writing, (cf. 'la pure amorce de ce chant', II, 1) is utterly new and foreign to him.

III

1. The omniscient voice of Poetry asserts the validity of the ascetic doctrine that one who gives up everything will 'inherit the earth'. III, 1–9 present poetic inspiration as a wave rolling through all history and geography and imposing itself in different ways on different poets (cf. love as an eternal force in *Amers*: 'Une même vague par le monde, une même vague depuis Troie roule sa hanche jusqu'à nous'). Note the heightened rhetoric of Inspiration, with denser linguistic texture than elsewhere despite similarities of repetitive devices, but at the same time her presentation as an integral part of the poet. One must not be drawn into the temptation of referring to this female characterisation of the voice of poetry as the Muse, with its inappropriate overtones from the Romantic poets. In a note to me, Perse declares: 'Il s'agit seulement de l'âme, de l'esprit, de la figuration même spirituelle qui accompagne et double le poète comme son ombre divine ou sacrale.'

2. *dénombrement de peuples en exode.* Although it is impossible for a reader not to think of the 1940 *exode* before the German invasion, it should not be forgotten that a census of exiles is by no means uncommon (e.g. the Book of Numbers).

tumulte. In sense of Latin *tumultus.*

gonflement de lèvres . . . e.g. Bible *verba* before being book.

3. *ébriété.* Roger Caillois (*Poétique de Saint-John Perse*, Gallimard, 1954, p. 142) notes that 'l'ivresse passe d'un coup de sa phase bénigne à sa phase écrasante'.

6. This line is often injudiciously used by critics to characterise Perse's poetry, whereas it is applied here to the unintelligible source of inspiration of which it is the poet's task to make sense by selection.

8. The relationship between inspiration and exile is here more closely defined. After rising to the heights of passion and desire, the gull's cry, symbolising the pursuing Furies, follows the poet relentlessly along the shore.

9. *numide.* Refers to the North African nomadic tribe of ancient times famous for their horsemanship; cf. VII, 10.

10. *monstre*. The insistent demands of inspiration. In letters to Mina Curtiss, Perse refers to ' "le monstre" en moi' (Pléiade, p. 1049) and asks: 'Que savons-nous des "monstres"?—leur mutisme' (p. 1044). Cf. Rimbaud: 'Ma camarade, mendiante, enfant monstre' (*Illuminations*, 'Phrases').

long débat. The continuous interior dialogue between the poet and the 'monstre' within him, between his will and his subconscious.

11. Note the insidiousness of inspiration.

14. *Mendiante*. A characterisation of the 'souffle originel'.

Prodigue. Cf. vii, 13; the poet himself.

15–16. The tables are finally turned; the poet accepts his duty and in so doing creates something positive out of a situation in which everything seemed negative. The wind plays its part in this decision by underlining the precariousness of the exile's position: its importance is more metaphysical than purely geographical.

17–23. The poet's inner voice takes up the threads of her earlier disquisition on the nature of poetic inspiration.

17. *clameur*. Taken up from iii, 1, 4, 7. The silent clamour is a spiritual one.

levée de siècles. Cf. 'haut fait d'armes', iii, 2.

18. *ïambe farouche*. Synecdoche for the poem. Claudel's concentration on 'l'ïambe fondamental, un temps faible et un temps fort' ('Réflexions et propositions sur le vers français') marked an important new direction in French versification. Perse developed this in his own way (see monograph pp. 99ff.). It might be noted that in Chénier's *Iambes*, political satires written during the Reign of Terror, reference is made to 'l'ïambe sanguinaire'. Because of the use of the iamb in Classical and English prosody, there is no reason to suppose that Perse had this in mind nor that he is associating the iamb with a particular kind of poetry (especially political satire).

19. *rive accore*. Nautical term for a sheer cliff.

19–20. *Saisisseur . . . Manieur . . . Nourrisseur*. The poet struggling with his inspiration on the threshold of day.

19. *glaives à l'aurore*. Cf. *Amers*, Strophe, ix, 6–1; '*avant l'aurore et les glaives du jour*'.

20. *aigres*. ' "Aigre" est ici pris, très concrètement, au sens *figuratif* et presque linéaire d'une suggestion d'ordre plastique, et non moral: dans le sens, purement visuel, d'"acéré", d'aigu, d'anguleux' (letter from Perse to R.L.); cf. *Vents* iv, 5: 'nos filles . . . s'aiguisent sous le casque.'

[*les*] *filles les plus aigres sous la plume de fer*. Cf. *Pour Dante*: 'Et l'aile acerbe du génie nous frôlera encore de sa plume de fer'. The concepts in these two phrases cancel out to leave the equation of 'filles' with 'génie', each

'fille' being therefore the inspiration for an individual poem. Cf. also the term 'fer aigre'.

21. Note Latin sense of 's'horripile' and 'orient'. On the progression of dawn expressed in the line, see Caillois, p. 62.

23. *le lieu de ma naissance*. Still within quotation marks, and so not a private question by Leger, but an unanswerable question by Inspiration.

IV

2. *grande fille répudiée*. The Mendiante of iii, 14 and iv, 13; called 'Partout-errante', iv, 4. Her dismissal at dawn is a logical imaginative consequence of the debate between the night of the subconscious and the day of the conscious will.

3. *les constellations labiles qui changent de vocable* . . . The principal meaning of 'labiles' here is 'falling', i.e. appearing to move downwards in the night sky. Its Latin origin (*labi* 'to change', 'to slip') allows the introduction of the linguistic imagery leading to 'la recherche du mot pur' through its double meaning: cf. *lapsus* in both French and English. But the principal sense of the line is that different parts of the night sky are seen from different continents. See also note to iv, 6.

4. *Partout-errante*. Cf. vii, 9.
Sibylles. Cf. 'Pluies', i, 6; 'Poème à l'Etrangère', iii, 4 and 17.
et le matin . . . Cf. ii, 19.

5. *Servantes*. The 'Sibylles' of 1.4: the Sibylline Books are incomprehensible, whence 'vaines'.
l'échéance. Note primacy of root meaning: cf. *Anabase* i: 'l'échéance de nos rives'.

6. *l'hyade pluvieuse*. One of the stars in the constellation Taurus (cf. iv, 3; and is there an echo of the 'Princes en Tauride', i, 7?), traditionally associated with rain when they are near the horizon at the equinoxes. Hyades = 'Rainy Ones' (< Gr. ὕειν). In the *Aeneid* (iii, 515–6), when Palinurus wakes to observe the night sky, the Hyades are mentioned with the equivalent epithet immediately after the 'sidera . . . labentia' (cf. 'constellations labiles', iv, 3):

> sidera cuncta notat tacito labentia caelo,
> Arcturum pluviasque Hyadas geminosque Triones . . .

7. *sur les rives très anciennes fut appelé mon nom*. Cf. iv, 2: Inspiration calling from the ancient shores of poetry.
l'esprit du dieu. Cf. i, 6.
l'inceste. In ancient Rome, sexual relationships with a Vestal were considered incestuous. Here there is the additional consideration that the relations between the Poet and Poetry are of the same order. Perse wrote to Claudel: 'L'art même, n'est à mon sens, qu'inceste entre

l'instinct et la volonté' (Pléiade, p. 1017), and in an early letter to Rivière had declared bluntly: 'Art = onanisme' (p. 668).

9. Cf. a less elliptical version of the same image in *Anabase* VII: 'et ces fumées de sable qui s'élèvent au lieu des fleuves morts, comme des pans de siècles en voyage'. The poet himself is the interpreter.

le ciel plein ... d'errantes prémisses. Cf. II, 18.

11. *style.* 'stylus' rather than 'style'.

13. *Mendiante.* Cf. III, 14.

antres. The cave recalls the setting for various mythological unions, but also seems totally appropriate for the 'illicit' union between the poet and his inspiration, being a reflection of the deep recesses of his mind in which the poem takes shape.

14. *signes.* Note Latin sense of 'constellations'; cf. II, 18, IV, 3.

15. *Ainsi va toute chair.* Larbaud's title for Butler's *The Way of All Flesh* which he translated in 1921. No connection, however, need be supposed.

sel. Symbol of purity (see monograph, pp. 106–7)

le fruit de cendre. Cf. IV, 7.

la rose naine de vos sables. Both a botanical reference and a transferred epithet similar to that in I, 4. A 'rose des sables' is a crystalline formation of gypsum found in deserts.

l'épouse nocturne. Claudel uses the same term for 'la Muse qui est la Grâce'.

15–17. See Caillois pp. 102–4. Through parallel phrasing it is made quite clear that the sacred prostitute is identified with the poet's writing.

16. *au van de la mémoire.* 'plus un poète avance dans le monde du mystère, ... plus il a besoin, dans cet écart, de sa mémoire et de sa volonté' (Pléiade, p. 1300). Note the importance of the present moment. *insane.* Formed on Latin root.

nautile. The thin, papery 'shell' of the argonaut or paper nautilus, an animal distantly related to an octopus, has a ribbed pattern on its white surface reminiscent of a sandy shore. The creature lives on the high seas, and its translucent 'shell' is actually an elaborate egg-case.

17. *l'aile fossile ...* Cf. *Amers*, Chœur, 2: *'l'ambre fossile et clair enchâssé d'ailes éphémères'.* André Chénier's metaphor for poetic creation (in 'L'Invention') as an insect trapped in amber ('Tombe odorante où vit [*sic*] l'insecte volatile [*sic*]', l. 248) is specifically repudiated by Perse, being opposed utterly to his aesthetics in which movement plays a central role.

vêpres. Both 'vespers' and 'evenings' (<hespera).

18. *à la pointe des sables.* Note the place chosen for the ritual purification. *plume ... ongle ... chevelures ... toiles impures.* Appurtenances destroyed in various magical ceremonies of purification. (cf. *Anabase*, III: 'On fait brûler la selle du malingre'.)

19. *de la cendre au lait*. Note the progression of connotation around 'cendre' (cf. lines 7 & 15), the impurities gradually being eradicated.

20. *sans office*. Cf. Baudelaire's view of the poem as a sufficient end in itself, with no material purpose.

21. *encore . . . un grand poème délébile*. The poem envisaged begins in canto v, and occupies the long sections between quotation marks right to the end of 'Exil'. It is an integral part of Perse's aesthetic that the value of poetry lies in activity: once the act of poetry has been performed, the poet moves on to his next act, while only the *active* reader will enjoy his poem as an essential ingredient of living fully.

V

1–8. An evocation of his own childhood with its simple sense of complete harmony with nature.

1. *casque*. As a child he wore a 'lourd chapeau de paille ou de soleil, coiffé d'une double feuille de siguine' ('Pour fêter une enfance', iv), and his father a pith-helmet ('Ecrit sur la porte', 'Pour fêter une enfance', vi).

2. *l'oreille à ces coraux*. It has the same effect as when we hold a sea-shell to our ear.

3. *ma rive natale*. Born in Guadeloupe, he is now back on the western coast of the Atlantic. But the meaning goes much deeper, as the rest of the line indicates.

4. *achaine*. Variant spelling of 'akène' (q.v. in *Petit Larousse*): the seed of certain fruit (e.g. strawberry).

5. *os creux*. A physiological fact which Perse develops in *Oiseaux*, 2: 'L'oiseau, sur ses os creux et sur ses "sacs aériens", porté, plus légèrement que chaume, à l'excellence du vol, défiait toutes notions acquises en aérodynamique . . .'
guifette. Sea-swallow.
eaux filles en vêtement d'écailles. The poet imagining himself swimming, conjures up mermaids at the sensual contact with the waves. Bachelard notes parallel ideas (*L'Eau et les rêves*, Corti, 1942, pp. 171–7).

6. *Ô sables, ô résines!* Note the syntactical and rhythmic echo of ii, 20 on the reintroduction of the idea of exile. The sands are not violent, being the key to mediation (cf. i, 2) but violence is done to the day, speared like a fish. The poet's meditation cannot help bringing images of aggression and sadness to his mind, recognising as it does the ephemeral nature of the joy and beauty he has evoked.

7. The repetition of 'merveille' should be taken as a sign of simplicity and strength.

8. The recognition of the ambiguity of life and particularly of its

transience and inadequacy stops the poet short with a metaphysical question. Cf. the crucial turning-point in *Vents*, IV, 3, and similar 'brink' questions: *Anabase*, VIII; *Amers*, Strophe, IV:

Que m'a donné le monde que ce mouvement d'herbes?
Où vint la chose à nous manquer, et le seuil quel est-il, que nous n'avons foulé?

9. *Je sais. J'ai vu.* The phrase is used again in *Amers*, Strophe, IX, 5–2, and may echo, though not consciously, the opening words of verses 8 and 9 in Rimbaud's 'Le Bateau ivre': both poets are claiming to have seen something and to have knowledge quite out of the ordinary.

10. The disparity of reference emphasises the wandering search.
Arsace. Founder of the Arsacid dynasty of Parthian kings in Mesopotamia. There is perhaps an echo of Racine's *Bérénice* in which another Arsace figures: 'Dans l'Orient désert quel devint mon ennui?' (Act I sc. iv).
euphorbe. Spurge has a bitter taste and indeed contains poison in its milky sap.

11. *Sahel.* Sahara, specifically the northern coastal region.
l'azalaïe. See Perse's letter to MacLeish (see above p. 88). In a letter to me of 18 March 1964 there is additional information: ' "Azalaïe":— Très vieux mot de langage indigène désignant, dans le monde musulman, la grande caravane annuelle du trafic du sel, qui joue un rôle traditionnel, quasi rituel, entre l'Afrique du Nord et les territoires d'Afrique Centrale.'

12. Both the 'Dark Ages' and perhaps the present century.

13. *sesterces.* With this Roman silver coinage, cf. 'deniers' (VI, 5h). Cf. the revelation of this treasure trove in V, 13. The image is principally one of colour, the bright visual effect of the sun evoking silver coins.

14. *O présides sous l'eau verte!* The submarine world seems imprisoned, in an exile of its own. Cf. the development of underwater imagery in 'Poème à l'Etrangère'.

15. *feuilles de calcaire.* The formations of coral on the reef.
masque de la mort. Cf. 'la tristesse soulève son masque de servante' ('Neiges', II, 4).

VI

NOTE. Because of the length of each *verset*, I have subdivided them here by breaking at each semi-colon and designating each unit by a letter (omitting i, l, and o to avoid possible confusion with numbers).

1–7. A wide variety of solitary occupations is listed: specialists in difficult tasks watching in various remote places over rare and fragile things, others needed in emergencies who have to keep their tools in good fettle, maintainers of purity in numerous ways, those intimately at one with nature, scientists engaged in remote pursuits dreamers fulfilling non-utilitarian needs. patrons and creative artists. Certain critics (e.g. André

Breton and Roger Garaudy) see the repeated 'Celui qui' as a levelling formula. It is no less, however, a designation of the specific and exceptional. Those evoked are all 'Princes de l'exil' with whom the poet feels a close kinship. Each verset has internal coherence. On the list see Caillois pp. 111–9, and intro. pp. 15–16.

1d. *celui qui laque en haute mer* . . . Traditionally the Chinese produce their finest lacquer objects at sea as the merest speck of dust will spoil the work. Perse refers to the practice in a letter to Joseph Conrad: 'Les dernières grandes familles de laqueurs chinois haïssaient d'avoir à vivre en mer, au large du Petchili, pour se garer des poussières du "vent jaune" ' (Pléiade, p. 887). And in 'Chanté par Celle qui fut là' he recalls 'les vieux laqueurs de Chine ont les mains rouges sur leurs jonques de bois noir'. Against such strong evidence, the tentative suggestion that Perse was recalling the Creole word *laker* 'to bait, to fish' (see my 'Saint-John Perse et le parler créole', *Revue des Sciences Humaines*, 139 (July–September 1970), 471) loses all its force.

2a. *flatte.* 'Soothes'.

3a. *l'amer.* Perse's only recorded usage of the word before *Amers*.

3b. *un lait pauvre.* sc. 'lait de chaux'.

cinéraires. The plants rather than the ashes, both 'cineraria' in English.

3f. *dérivation.* In the nautical sense of 'drift'.

3g. *l'argile rouge des grands fonds.* Perse had originally written 'l'argile mauve des grands fonds' and explains the change to Roger Caillois: 'il s'agit bien d'une véritable correction, non d'une "variante". Précision de fait, imposée par l'océanographie. (Precision d'ailleurs inattendue pour l'imagination première, qui n'associe point d'elle-même le rouge à la nuit abyssale. —Je n'ai jamais moi-même, de mes yeux, vu que l'argile *mauve* des hauts fonds, rapportée à bout de sonde ou de patte d'ancre dans les mouillages côtiers d'un marin amateur. D'où le mécanisme inconscient d'une fausse association.)' (Pléiade, p. 563).

4c. *feux de ronces.* Cf. *Anabase* x (also in an enumeration and also connected with death): 'les feux de ronces et d'épines aux lieux souillés de mort.'

4f. *lieu d'ossuaires et d'égouts.* Cf. *Vents* ii, 2, 'En lieux jonchés de lances et de navettes d'os . . . ' and ii, 5: 'un lieu de poudres et d'esquilles . . . ' Perse's predilection for such unpromising, deserted places serves to emphasise his positive achievements: cf. *Vents* i, 2: 'Le Narrateur monte aux remparts dans la fraîcheur des ruines et gravats.'

5c. *Offices des . . . Tabacs.* Tobacco is a state monopoly in France. 'Offices' is not the usual French word for any of these administrative centres, although used for others.

5d. *où gisent les fables.* Note the effect of giving the yarns material substance.

5h. *haras*. France has state stud-farms (e.g. beside the famous abbey at Cluny, and in Normandy).

ténèbres. Cf. the connection between horses and shadow in *Anabase* VII: 'mon âme tout enténébrée d'un parfum de cheval'.

6a. *à la boucle d'un fleuve*. Although Bordeaux where Perse studied lies on a bend in the Garonne, there is no specific evidence that he has a particular town in mind; rather is he creating an imaginary town with features common to many.

6e. *le haut peigne sonore des grands barrages de montagne*. A splendidly exact synæsthetic image.

6g. *le parvis des grands convulsionnaires*. The cemetery of Saint-Médard church in Paris was the meeting place for Jansenist fanatics and miracles were said to happen, provoking hysterical convulsions in some of the participants. 'Convulsionnaires' nonetheless exist in many communities (e.g. the 'Holy Rollers' of Maine whom Perse mentions, Pléiade, p. 905).

7e. *Baber*. The first Great Moghul (1482–1530), famous both for his military exploits and literary capacities.

7f. *au tympan sont telles cruches, comme des ouïes, murées pour l'acoustique*. In Gothic churches one sometimes finds pitchers set into the walls for acoustic purposes. (I know of an instance in the Chartreuse at Villeneuve-lès-Avignon.) The American translation has another reading, followed by Otten: 'there are crockets in the spandrel, like ears, walled in for the acoustics'. This seems a highly suspect interpretation since the acoustics would not be affected.

7m. The items in brackets are indeed used in the calculation of moveable feasts: see the appropriate tables in the Book of Common Prayer.

7p. Coming as it does after references to religion and language, this final item cannot help evoking the legend of Moses, himself the leader of a 'peuple en exode' (see III, 2), receiving the tablets of stone on Mount Sinai, but Perse is thinking rather of any man subject to the divine spark of inspiration who thereby becomes a natural lawgiver of mankind. Stones polished by lightning are common enough on mountain tops.

8. *princes de l'exil*. Cf. II, 9 and Baudelaire, 'Les Litanies de Satan'.

'O Prince de l'exil, à qui l'on a fait tort,

Et qui, vaincu, toujours se redresse plus fort.'

9. *Etranger, sur toutes grèves de ce monde* represents a subtle expansion of the refrain phrase: 'Et, sur toutes grèves de ce monde'.

Ponant: 'West' (cf. 'Levant'). Normally applied to the Mediterranean, it is used here rather of America.

porte à l'oreille . . . une conque. Cf. V, 2.

10. Note the precarious stance of the poet at the threshold: his values are rejected.

le seuil des Lloyds. The insurance interests of the firm are well known, but there seems to be some grammatical confusion here, the possessive (Lloyd's) being changed to a plural.

11. *J'habiterai mon nom*. Leger's pseudonym is of considerable importance to him, allowing a separation of functions between public and private life. Cf. Oscar Wilde's less modest statement when asked by the U.S. customs what he had to declare: 'Nothing but my genius'. Cf., more seriously, Shakespeare's *Richard II* where the king's loss of identity is complete when he no longer has even a name to exist in (see esp. IV, i, 255 ff.): 'I have no name, no title/ . . . And know not now what name to call myself!'

12. The storm reveals different coins from those buried earlier by the sun (V, 13). The image of poetic fulguration here suggests the value attached by the poet to the '*grandes monnaies de fer*' which are not common currency in the everyday commerce of '*les tables du changeur*'.

VII

1. *l'autre rive*. That of France, across the Atlantic, but cf. V, 3.

2. *deux . . . femmes*. One is his mother, 'mère du Proscrit' (to whom 'Neiges' is to be dedicated) and the other the 'épouse' of VII, 8, then figuring in his life (he did not marry until 1958). Perse's discretion in such private matters raises to the universal plane ordinary relationships which in another writer's treatment could well be reduced to the trivial or anecdotal.

3. *arbre de phosphore*. Branching lightning.
orante. Normally applied to the statu(ett)e of a praying figure. Perse is here revivifying the Latin root.

6. cf. II, 20.
oiseau de Barbarie. The *tourterelle* or *colombe poignardée* which has a slash of blood red on its throat feathers. It will be remembered that Apollinaire devoted a *calligramme* to it, indicating the slash by a capital C. It is a poignant symbol of stricken tenderness.

9–10. The constant presence in the poet's mind of his tenderest feelings towards those he has left in France (see VII, 2) must not be allowed to distract him from his resolve.

9. *Partout errante*. Cf. IV, 4.

10. *ma course de Numide*. Cf. III, 10: 'mon âme numide'.

11. *Le nitre et le natron sont thèmes de l'exil*. Both substances are used for cleansing and so pertain to the ritual purification of exile. Natron is natural soda, used in mummification in ancient Egypt; 'nitre' is also saltpetre and so connected with the discharges of the lightning: the themes of nothingness and inspiration are also those of Perse's poem, and

so 'thèmes de l'exil'. Mixed with sand, the substances are subjected to intense heat and fuse to make glass: cf. the images of sand and glass in I, 3 & 4.

pistes osseuses Cf. I, 5, 'l'ossuaire des saisons'. The idea of death and nothingness is trodden underfoot.

l'éclair. Cf. I, 7; VII, I etc.

12. *Ceux-là qui furent . . .* Cf. II, 10. The Conquistadors (cf. *Vents*, III, I). Cf. note to 'Pluies', III, 4.

cornes. cf. II, 2. One cannot help recalling the trumpets made of ram's horn used by Joshua before the walls of Jericho nor that the blast of trumpets sounded on the Roman senate's declaration of war, when the gates of Mars guarded by Janus were opened (cf. I, I), went by the name of 'cornua' (e.g. *Aeneid*, VII, 607–15). But horns have been so widely used as trumpets in so many different societies that it is unwise to restrict the reference.

13. *Prodigue.* Cf. III, 14.

le sel et l'écume. Cf. II, 15.

Juin. 'Exil' was dated June 1941 in the first editions.

14. Note ritualistic lustration, purification of threshold.

15. *décliner.* 'To state'. The meaning is unambiguous despite suggestions by some critics that the word is as polyvalent as in the last line of the 'Chanson de Roland'. The process of purgation is complete, and a clear declaration of all the poet possesses (cf. 'J'habiterai mon nom' VI, II) is a necessary preliminary to his new life. He is at last free to declare his real name in all senses.

'PLUIES'

Dedication: Francis Biddle (1886–1968) and his wife Katherine (1890–); the former Attorney General of the United States (1941–5) and close friend of the poet; the latter, under her maiden name Katherine Garrison Chapin, has written a number of articles on Perse, giving certain biographical details useful to an understanding of the American poems.

I

1. *Le banyan de la pluie.* A brilliant visual image expressive of the shafts of rain; cf. VIII, I.

2. The starting-point of the image is possibly that of cumulus piling into thunder, but foam on a reef is linked with 'l'écume aux lèvres du poème' (II, 6); cf. notes to 'Exil' II, 15.

lait d'eau vive. Cf. 'un lait de coraux' (II, 6) and 'lait de chaux vive', 'Exil' II, 15. Coral consists of lime deposits, and the sea is whipped into foam on the reef.

3. *l'Idée*. Cf. II 8. Nakedness and weaponry are associated with the Idea behind the poem on both occasions. These are also attributes of the rain. The 'Idée' is not the Muse (since it is to teach the poet 'le rite et la mesure contre l'impatience du poème', II, 9) but the idea of using the rains as an ambivalent image in the organisation of the poem. Charles Dolamore writes of the personified 'Idée': 'Perhaps we can say she is the essence of the rains; she appears to intercede between the thing itself and its expression in poetic terms, marrying the formless onslaught of the rains with the more exacting form of the artistic creation.' ('The Love and Aggression of SJP's "Pluies" ', *Forum for Modern Language Studies*, VII, 3, July 1971, 212).

peigne . . . sa crinière. Cf. V, 8: the action of combing the hair is connected with rain-making in various primitive communities (see e.g. J. G. Frazer, *The Golden Bough*, III, *Taboo and the Perils of the Soul*. p. 271).

5. *l'évasion*. The echo of 'évaser' is inescapable.

6. *Vierges prophétiques*. Cf. 'Sibylles' ('Exil' IV, 4, 'Poème à l'Etrangère', III, 4 and 17). The rain is the virgin (cf. I, 11) inspiring the poet and descending for union with the earth.

8. *ô fraude*. The contrast with '*un tel songe*' suggests that Perse is here expressing the habit of human deception which is to be exposed to the purifying force of the rain in canto VII.

9. *la rose obscène du poème*. The 'mystic rose' at the inspirational heart of poetry invites caution: measure, imposed by the poet's ordering intelligence, is an essential counterbalance. The 'obscene' rose is to be mastered in the course of the poem and the sexual implications developed: cf. VI, 6; VIII, 9.

10. *Seigneur terrible de mon rire* is a recurrent refrain in the poem: cf. I, 13; II, 10 and 11; IX, 3 and 4. It is another form of the 'Idée' (cf. the similarity of II, 9 and 10), its implications of majestic power and overt enjoyment being similarly paralleled by the image of the rain, also expressive both of power and joy, of destruction and regeneration.

11. *l'argile veuve*. Firstly the earth itself, then 'human clay' (cf. VI, 13; VII, 1).

hommes insomnieux. 'Pluies' was apparently written at night (see C. Ogburn, 'Comment fut écrit "Pluies" ', *Honneur*, pp. 273–9) and Perse is writing 'un chant du large pour qui veille' (VI, 15).

12. *la perte de mémoire*. Cf. IV, 11; V, 4; VII, 5. It is something desirable in Perse's ethics and aesthetics.

14. *l'étagement des mers*. Cf. 'une mer . . . / étagée comme un ciel au-dessus des vergers' ('Pour fêter une enfance', V) and Rimbaud:

'la mer étagée là-haut comme sur les gravures' (*Illuminations*, 'Après le déluge'). There are other apparent echoes of Rimbaud's prose poem, both in the image of the effects of the Flood and in the personification of the rain as 'la Reine, la Sorcière' who is silent since 'l'idée du Déluge se fut rassise' ('*l'idée* du Déluge', note, not simply 'le Déluge': cf. 1, 3); failing any longer to enjoy poetic insight, which the Flood had inspired, Rimbaud, unlike Perse, succumbs to 'ennui'. By none of this do I wish to suggest, however, that Perse consciously used Rimbaud's poem as a starting-point: there is simply a chance parallelism stemming from similar preoccupations.

15. *l'heure nouvelle*. The stress on renewal is an important feature of the poem.

II

1. The successive attributes of the rain are variously personified in some striking plurals: Nourrices and Suivantes, here; Sœurs, Guerrières, Danseuses, armes, filles, aigles, vierges, gerbes (III); Nourrices, Semeuses, Simoniaques (IV); Transfuges, Mimes, Métisses (VI); laveuses (VII). All but 'Transfuges' and 'Mimes' are feminine.

2. *à qui*. Sc. 'à celui qui'.

4. *l'Ande sur mon toit*. Gives the idea of powerful mass rising high above the poet's roof and so expresses everything which soars above man's earthly domain into the vaster realm of the unknown.

6. *l'écume aux lèvres du poème*. Cf. Mallarmé: 'Rien, cette écume, vierge vers' ('Salut'); the phrase is taken up in VIII, 13. Cf. also the significance of 'écume' in 'Exil' (e.g. II, 15).

7. *psylle*. A word generalised to mean 'snake-charmer' from the special capacities of the Psylli, a North African tribe. Cf. a phrase from Perse's tribute to Léon-Paul Fargue: 'il fut toujours assez intelligent pour tenir l'intellect à la porte du poème' (in L.-P. F., *Poésies*, Gallimard, 1963, p. 8).

8. *L'Idée*. Cf. I, 3.

9. The poet's controlling hand must always be uppermost despite the temptations.

10. Note Perse's refusal of facility.

12. *fraudes consumées*. Cf. I, 8.

13. *la nuit claire de midi*. A paradox, whose resolution allows special insight into 'l'essence de l'être' (II, 14). The image might derive from the visual effect of heavy rain-clouds darkening the sky.

14. *Ô fumées*. Expressive, as often in Perse, of urban civilisation with its overtones of creature comforts and the pollution the rains are to

wash away. Note how 'l'être' and 'l'âtre', so similar in sound, represent opposite poles in Perse's dialectic.

15. *la pluie tiède.* Rain falling through warm air feels warm at the beginning of a storm: gradually it cools, so that later in the poem the word 'fraîcheur' is associated with the rain.

III

1. *Sœurs des guerriers d'Assur.* On surviving monuments, ranks of tall, hieratic Assyrian warriors are familiar figures. Perse is stressing the slender power of the shafts of rain.

3. Dido was abandoned by her conquering lover Aeneas, and deluded by his promises, the gates of ivory being indicative of delusion (see Homer, *The Odyssey,* XIX, 562 ff). Perse's fondness for music might suggest that he was familiar with the famous episode more through Berlioz's *The Trojans* than from the *Aeneid* itself.

4. Marina, Cortes's mistress and interpreter, was also left behind when he returned to Europe. MacLeish's best-known poem, 'Conquistador', which won him the Pulitzer Prize in 1932, deals with Cortes. The story is none the less available to be referred to directly: one need not take this as a veiled tribute to the dedicatee of 'Exil'. Perse finds it regrettable that such references and even individual words should be distorted by the limitations of a particular reader's bookish learning.

plantes apocryphes. May refer to the Aztec tradition of creating pictures with feathers (see e.g. G.C. Vaillant, *The Aztecs of Mexico,* Harmondsworth, 1950, plate 45).

6. *l'Avril.* Cf. VIII, 6; it is immaterial that the month does not square with that given by Ogburn for the poem's composition (November). April is connected both with seasonal rainfall and with the renewal of the life-forces of spring, the regeneration of the earth.

8–9. *Guerrières . . .* The warlike attributes of the rain are completed by the winning charm of 'Danseuses', the inseparability of the two characteristics being underlined by the parallel phrasing of the *versets.*

13. *la science aux bouches des fontaines.* Oracular knowledge.

14. *les grandes affiches annonaires.* Note the link, through the image of the harvest, with the rains seen as 'gerbes non liées! l'ample et vive moisson' two lines before. For *annonaires,* see *Petit Larousse* s.v. 'annone'.

IV

1. *Edile* continues the references to the Roman Empire: cf. 'rétiaire' (I, 3); 'Vierges prophétiques' (I, 6); 'psylle' (II, 7); 'factions' (II, 8) if Knodel's reading in his book (p. 77) as 'charioteer-factions' is correct;

'Didon' (III, 3) by association; 'distribution d'aigles aux légions' (III, 10); 'bas-empire' (IX, 1, see note).

9. *les plus beaux êtres*. Perse's fondness for birds receives full expression in *Oiseaux*.

11. *si bas qu'on en perde mémoire*. Cf. I, 12.

12. The sacred nature of the rain is presented.

13. *au frais commerce de l'embrun*. 'Contre l'acception courante et maritime du mot "embruns" (au pluriel), "l'embrun" ici est pris au sens premier et général (peu usité) du mot au singulier: brume fraîche du ciel. Toute l'évocation du poème est d'ambiance terrestre: ville dans les terres et non port maritime (en fait, Savannah . . .)' Letter from Perse to R.L., 16 December 1965.

V

1. *nos maigres scories*. Burnt waste materials often exemplify man's' terrestrial condition in Perse: cf. 'cendres' ('Exil', VI, 1d), 'fumées' (II, 14 etc.)

3. *notre instance humaine*. 'instance' is best taken in its legal sense, 'Série des actes d'une procédure ayant pour objet de saisir un tribunal d'une contestation, d'instruire la cause et d'obtenir un jugement' (*Petit Larousse*), but see Dolamore for a variant view. The legal imagery of 'Pluies' is introduced by 'assises' in the opening line.

4. The elliptical presentation brings one up with a start, but the syntax is quite clear; cf. Mallarmé: 'Réflechissons . . . / ou si les femmes . . .' ('L'Après-midi d'un faune').

5. *la taie sur l'oeil* prepares us for the extensive use of the phrase in canto VII.
voilà-t-il pas beaux thèmes. Further ellipsis, the omission of 'de' compensating, from the point of view of register, for the astonishingly colloquial 'voilà-t-il pas'.

6. *invalide*. Cf. Latin 'invalidus'. Note use of generic, abstract noun where the individual, concrete one might be expected: 'enfance', 'veuvage'.

15. The pattern *J'avais, j'avais ce goût* . . . is repeated in VI, 3 and 12, and echoed in the reiterated *Lavez, lavez* of canto VII.

VI

1. *Un homme atteint de telle solitude*. A stronger presentation of the 'homme très seul' of 'Poème à l'Etrangère', III.

2. *je portais l'éponge et le fiel*. Seems an echo of the final gesture to Christ before his death (see e.g. Matthew xxvii, 34 and 48). In view of the

repeated phrase 'la taie sur l'œil' (v, 5; vii, 3) however, and of the reference to Tobias and the Angel in 'Poème à l'Etrangère' (iii, 19), it might be of interest to recall the Book of Tobit in the Apocrypha, 6, 8: 'The gall [of the 'big fish' Tobias has just caught] is for anointing a man's eyes when white patches have spread over them, or for blowing on the white patches in the eyes; the eyes will then recover' (*New English Bible*). Tobias does in fact cure his father's blindness with the remedy.

6. Cf. i, 9.

9. The Sphinx is traditionally associated with riddles (cf. *Oedipus Rex*): the Rains are loth to give up the secret of their origins.

12. A succinct statement of the exiled poet's position: his dream softens his bitterness; the images of beach and rain force him to modify his view.

13. *Passez . . . et nous laissez.* Perse approves the elegant archaic turn for a double imperative, cf. 'Allez et nous laissez . . .' ('Poème pour Valery Larbaud, "Jadis Londres . . ." ') and 'Allez et vous penchez . . .' ('Adresse du Poète . . .').

VII

1. *Innombrables sont nos voies.* Cf. Pindar, *Isthmian Ode* 4, first line: 'Multitudinous are the ways the gods have given' (tr. R. Lattimore). *Tel s'abreuve au divin . . .* Cf. vi, 13. *eaux-mères.* Perse implies both the strict chemical sense and a broader imaginative meaning based on that of the component words.

4. *la souillure du langage sur les lèvres publiques.* Cf. Isaiah 6, 5: 'I am a man of unclean lips, and I dwell in the midst of a people of unclean lips'. Perse's meaning is probably more immediate, however: let those in positions of authority not debase language. *la main basse.* The humiliating hand of the abusive tyrant.

5. *Cahiers du Tiers-Etat.* The lists of grievances presented by the commoners to the leaders of the French Revolution. *Lavez . . . les hautes tables de mémoire.* Cf. i, 12; iv, 11; v, 4.

6. *les phrases les mieux faites, les pages les mieux nées.* Cf. 'Exil' ii, 4. Perse makes a distinction between 'faire' and 'naître' much like that between Valéry's 'vers donnés' and 'vers calculés'. *le sel de l'atticisme.* The essence of Greek culture (not to be confused with 'le sel attique' = 'raillerie délicate et fine'). *la litière du savoir.* Perse wrote of this: 'J'ai bien voulu évoquer la litière d'étable, d'écurie, en acceptant tout ce que peut engager de péjoratif l'ambiguïté du mot (détritus ou déchets)'. (Letter to R.L., 16 December 1965).

VIII

1. Cf. i, 1.

6. *Pluies en marche sous le fouet.* Cf. 'Exil', vii, 13, where the lightning is a whip.

un Ordre de Flagellants. Religious fanatics of the late Middle Ages given to public flagellation.

8. *l'Avril.* Cf. iii, 6.

9. From being 'la terre au goût de vierge noire' (viii, 7), the earth is now 'au goût de femme faite femme'.

10. *mille glaives.* Cf. the 'glaive' of 'l'Idée' offered by the rain (ii, 9).

sacres. Sakers, a kind of falcon.

aux vasques des fontaines. Cf. iii, 13.

11. *la truie d'or à bout de stèle.* Perhaps an echo of the Israelites' false god, the golden calf.

12. Note how the rains reawaken desire even in those to whom it is forbidden by normal mores to realise their natural instincts.

13. Cf. ii, 6.

14. *idées nouvelles.* Cf. v, 9.

15. *mon poème . . . qui ne fut pas écrit.* Cf. 'Exil' iv, 21.

IX

1. *bas-empire des taillis.* An extraordinary application of the idea of decadence connected with the late Roman Empire, with overtones of the 'dark ages', to a copse. The Roman references in the poem (see note to iv, 1) appropriately end with this oblique allusion.

2. Cf. ii, 5.

au fléau de l'esprit. The preceding phrase, 'Et toutes choses égales', suggests for 'fléau' the meaning of 'balance-arm'. It seems not, therefore, to echo the 'pestilences de l'esprit' of 'Exil' ii, 15.

3. *l'esclandre* (< Lat. scandalum) like 'scandale' and 'mensonge' seems to have no pejorative tone for Perse.

4. The refrain line '*Seigneur terrible de mon rire*' is finally broken down and some of its components presented separately.

au seuil aride du poème. Note the contrast to the preceding deluge.

les paons verts de la gloire. The strutting of peacocks is most apt as an image of those who seek public recognition. 'Gloire' retains something of its seventeenth-century sense of 'boastfulness'. In some parts of the Far East (e.g. Burma), green peacocks symbolise the sun.

'NEIGES'

Dedication: Françoise-Renée Saint-Léger Léger, née Dormoy (†1948), mother of the poet.

I

1. *Et puis* . . . The opening underlines the sense of continuity, the poem representing as it were only an episode in a broader sequence. 26 of the 63 sentences in 'Neiges' begin with 'Et'.

lés. Cf. IV, 4 ('navettes d'os', 'amande d'ivoire'), IV, 5 ('nous tissera linge', 'lés du songe').

hommes de mémoire as opposed to Perse himself who relishes 'la simple chose d'être là' ('Exil', V, 4).

sous le sel gris. An example of paronomasia provoking the reader to include 'ciel' in his reading of 'sel'.

un lieu de grâce et de merci. Cf. IV, 4. Introduces the religious imagery of the poem.

grandes odes du silence. The oxymoron is to be exemplified by the poem.

2. *les hautes villes de pierre ponce forées d'insectes lumineux.* The poem was written in New York. The image of skyscrapers at night with some windows showing a light is brilliantly expressed by this phrase.

dans l'oubli de leur poids. An optical illusion is created by the snow falling evenly around the skyscrapers: these seem to be soaring upwards (cf. 'fusée' I, 3).

3. *cette heure soyeuse.* Silk represents to Perse whatever is most fragile and delicate (cf. 'Exil' II, 10, 'Neiges' II, 2). Cf. the weaving image of I, 1, and IV, 5.

Note how this extended verset is both closed in on itself through the similar first and last phrases and open through its enjambement to the next as well as being an extension of the previous one.

4. *transe.* Retains something of its Latin origins.

l'aube muette . . . enflait son corps de dahlia blanc. The precision of this multiple visual image is remarkable. The equivalence of snow to falling feathers, suggested first in line 2, is here expanded to a white owl puffing out its plumage like some great white dahlia with its layers of petals resembling the bird's feathers. But as usual, Perse goes beyond the visual: the silence of the owl is of the same order as that of the 'grandes odes du silence' (I, 1), and the bird swells with the insufflation of some invisible power of inspiration. The immateriality of the snow could not be better conveyed.

l'Architecte. The reminiscence of an actual event in the poet's life. He would be much attracted by the discovery of a timid bird's nest in such apparently inhospitable surroundings as the New York skyscrapers. The capital letter helps generalise the occurrence.

des œufs d'engoulevent. The celebrated whippoorwill, popularly supposed to suck the milk of goats (hence its other name, goatsucker). They would need to be pointed out as their camouflage of brown and greenish patches makes them difficult to spot in their rudimentary nests.

II

1. *ce naissain pâle*. This underwater image for the snow prepares for the 'nacres' of II, 2. Note also the echo of 'naissance'.

meuglement de bêtes sourdes. The paradox of 'odes du silence' is continued in the ships' sirens bellowing like dumb beasts.

aux chutes des grands fleuves. From the reference in II, 2 to the Great Lakes one thinks here of the Niagara Falls.

noctuelles. Owlet-moths; Lat. *noctua* 'night-owl' (cf. I, 4).

2. *très grands lacs*. The Great Lakes, around which industry is indeed concentrated.

haute treille sidérale. 'L'image symbolique de la neige, c'est l'étoile' (Durand, art. cit., p. 633).

choses grèges de la neige. As 'grège' is not often detached in French from the expression 'soie grège', cf. 'cette heure soyeuse' (I, 3).

3. *neige plus fine qu'au désert la graine de coriandre*. Cf. Exodus xvi, 31, where Manna is described: 'it was like coriander seed, white'. Coriander is of the family of umbelliferae: cf. IV, 4, 'Fraîcheur d'ombelles'.

4. *abiès*. Scientific (Latin) name for fir-trees.

vos deux mains congédiées. Seasonally out of work.

quelle inquiétante douceur. This sentence conveys beautifully, in Knodel's words, 'the strange and almost embarrassing gentleness of snow' (art. cit., p. 13).

Epouse du monde ma présence . . . The first appearance of an important refrain.

un songe de mélèze. One of the few deciduous conifers, larch has a delicacy appropriate to this evocation.

III

1. Notice the interplay of spatial and temporal elements in this stanza.

ce plain-chant des neiges. Religious imagery is taken up for expansion in this canto. Perse finds an equivalent in sound to the visual images he had developed in canto I.

neiges prodigues de l'absence. Note the ambiguity: these 'premières neiges de l'absence' (I, 1) are plentiful, but are also creative of a sense of absence.

2. *Celle.* His mother, to whom the poem is dedicated. (With her attitude of prayer cf. 'l'orante', 'Exil', vii, 3). After her death in October 1948, Perse wrote: 'C'est une profonde tristesse sur laquelle se referme mon cœur, et ma solitude s'en trouve grandement accrue. A ce cœur de mère je devais tout ce que j'ai pu garder de foi dans la nature humaine' (Pléiade, p. 948).

un pur lignage, notre race. Perse's sense of caste is clearly displayed here: it is one based on honour and generosity rather than on social status. The word 'pur', occurring six times in the last two cantos, defines the aim of his human and poetic quest in 'Neiges', 'lignage' and 'langage' being linked in both sound and sense.

ce langage sans paroles. Cf. 'un pur langage sans office', 'Exil', iv, 20. The reference anticipates the extended disquisition on the *Ursprache* of canto iv. In an explanation to Jean Paulhan, Perse wrote: 'Simple communication muette entre deux êtres: "langage", et non "langue", de fils à mère. Je n'ai jamais cru suggérer nulle part cette absurdité, que le poète, écrivant, pût s'exprimer sans "mots"; mais seulement qu'il associât, intégralement et unanimement, l'esprit et la lettre, le "langage" et le "mot", par décharge de tout l'être dans une même fulguration, inconsciente et consciente' (Pléiade, p. 582).

ô vous toute présence. 'Présence' and 'attente' are both characteristics of the 'Epouse du monde' (see ii, 4; iii, 6; iv, 2 & 5) which relates primarily to the snow but also by implication to the poet's mother and so to the nature of language itself.

un grand Ave *de grâce.* Sc. Ave Maria; cf. iv, 4, where the purity of the snow replaces that of the '*chant très pur de notre race*'.

3. *pays captif.* Occupied France.

grande pitié des femmes . . . à qui le bras des hommes fit défaut. A letter to MacLeish reveals some personal details behind this general statement: 'Je suis à bout d'insomnie et porte depuis dix jours les pires blessures que j'aie reçues dans ma solitude: mauvaises nouvelles au sujet de ma mère, un beau-frère menacé, un autre disparu, des neveux internés on ne sait où, de nouvelles spoliations contre celle de mes sœurs dont on a pu savoir encore quelque chose, et la déportation en Allemagne d'un être très cher qui avait le courage de veiller pour moi sur ma mère, d'assister moralement et matériellement ceux des miens à qui je fais maintenant défaut comme homme. Je me cogne en vain la tête à tous les murs, à la recherche de vaines formules. C'est bien la pire torture pour un homme, de ne pouvoir, pratiquement, rien pour des êtres, pour des femmes, qui dépendent entièrement de lui, et pour qui son nom même est néfaste' (Pléiade, p. 943; cf. p. 901).

Églises souterraines. The crypts and catacombs (centres of Resistance) where for many reasons lights would be kept low.

l'abeille, divine. In addition to the traditional symbolism of the bee, Perse attaches it to various forms of intellection (see my 'Language as Imagery in Saint-John Perse'). In the present religious context, it is reasonable to see it, with Knodel, as 'a reference to the promise of resurrection' but unnecessary to go as far as Monique Parent (*Saint-John Perse et quelques devanciers*, p. 238) and suggest the poem was written at Candlemas.

4. *aux roses pâles des ronciers j'ai vu pâlir l'usure de vos yeux.* A fine visual image associating the veining of wild rose flowers with that in the whites of tired eyes.

mutisme. Note its difference from 'silence': it is 'une pierre noire', an imposed state and so unproductive. Cf. the distinction between loneliness and solitude.

que veille en nous cette affre de douceur. Note the development from '*que veille en moi . . .*' (III, 2); cf. a similar change in IV, 5: 'épouse du monde notre attente'.

5. *aphtes.* The white scales which flake off in foot and mouth disease ('fièvre aphteuse').

gens de gabelle. The 'gabelle' was specifically the salt-tax of the Ancien Régime. Knodel suggests the idea here is rather that of 'persons working around the salt marshes and salt storehouses, where unrefined piles of salt would be reminiscent of slightly sullied snow' (art. cit., p. 12, n. 6). Salt is seen as a pure life-force in Perse's work. Cf.: 'Le sel, au dire de Hugo von Hofmannsthal, aura hanté toute mon œuvre de poète: principe même ou résidu de son activité. (Enfant, rêvant de France à travers La Fontaine, ce n'est point d'Eaux et Forêts, de Fermiers généraux ou d'Officiers de louveterie que je rêvais, ni d'une belle vie aux champs . . ., mais d'une simple carrière d'Officier de gabelle.) Adossé maintenant au loin à ces pyramides de sel blanc, je fais le compte de mes biens et m'élève, en ces lieux, contre toute menace d'excessive langueur' (Pléiade, p. 1061).

6. *un oiseau de cendre rose, qui fut de braise tout l'été.* There are many birds which enjoy a seasonal change of coloration. Here Perse is thinking of the cardinal bird which he also evokes in 'Poème à l'Etrangère', II, 9.

l'Oiseau du Phase. The Phasian bird, i.e. the pheasant, introduced to the West according to legend by Jason on his return from the River Phasis. It frequently figures in illuminated manuscripts.

l'An Mille. The Millennium was a particularly troubled period with fears for the end of the world. The bird is a ray of brightness and hope and in both cases embodies Perse's optimism for a better Spring.

mensonge. The word does not here have its usual pejorative overtones. The snow is a kind of illusion. Jean Schlumberger records that Perse 'n'attache aucune idée de défaveur au mensonge' ('Rencontres', *NRF*,

August 1967, p. 270), and in an early letter to Gustave-Adolphe Monod (Pléiade, p. 658), Leger wrote: 'il n'y a pas d'"art" sans *du* mensonge (initial ou subordonné, mais toujours assistant); ou du moins, en art, c'est au mensonge que la sincérité emprunte la plus sublime des maïeutiques.'

IV

1. *détacherai-je mon lit bas comme une pirogue.* A not unfamiliar reverie of which Bachelard gives an example: 'Mon divan est une barque perdue sur les flots ... Dors dans la tempête ..., heureux d'être un homme assailli par les flots' (*La Poétique de l'espace*, p. 43).

remontant les fleuves vers leur source. The image of navigation starts turning, on the word 'remontant', to the historical and physical exploration of language pursued in the next stanzas. Notice, however, how the two image patterns continue to run parallel for some time.

2. *dont la conduite est incertaine et la démarche est aberrante.* Cf. I, 2: '*dont la mémoire est incertaine et le récit est aberrant*'. The connection with the new moon underlines the element of uncertainty as well as of rebirth. It is a coincidence that equivalent phrasing of the image may be found in Apollonius Rhodius (*Argonautica*, IV, 1477 ff) and in Virgil (*Aeneid*, VI, 453–4).

3. *ces langues dravidiennes qui n'eurent pas de mot distinct pour "hier" et pour "demain".* Perse writes: 'Mon autorité là était celle de Pelliot, qui avait, avec Stael-Holstein et Granet, discuté devant moi cette question avec un Japonais, à Pékin, en 1918. Se rappelant l'intérêt que j'avais paru attacher à la question, Pelliot m'en avait reparlé à Paris, et passant à Washington après la deuxième guerre, il m'avait fait lire à ce sujet, dans une revue d'Orientalistes, un mémoire scientifique dont je pourrais retrouver l'auteur. Mais l'intérêt pour moi n'est pas le point d'érudition: c'est le fait qu'une langue humaine, quelle qu'elle fût, ait pu comporter, tout à la fois, et cette extension et cette contraction de l'esprit' (Pléiade, p. 581).

ce pur délice sans graphie. Cf. 'ce langage sans paroles', III, 2. Perse is concerned in 'Neiges' with seeking and establishing dynamically the limits of language. Despite some verbal echoes of Mallarmé ('pur délice sans chemin' in 'Autre éventail') and of Valéry ('Je remonte à la source où cesse même un nom' in 'Le Rameur'), he is not seeking the static crystallisation in the ineffable which seems to be their extra-literary goal, and which means that their practice can never attain to the aims of their theory, but full coverage of the range of human apprehension and expression. See also note to IV, 6.

jusqu'à ces locutions inouïes ou l'aspiration recule au-delà des voyelles. 'Nulle idée ici de langage, ou pré-langage sonore, encore inarticulé. Je n'ai jamais pensé qu'à l'aspiration initiale, marquée d'un signe indicatif dans beaucoup de langues encore vivantes et des plus articulées, des plus évoluées même, du proche et du lointain Orient, où l'émission, l'éjection du mot sous sa première consonne est amorcée, frappée plus que d'une simple intonation: d'une véritable accentuation en recul du souffle— le contraire d'un amuïssement' (Pléiade, pp. 580–1). The quest for the source of language seems to designate an *Ursprache*, the pure spring from which many languages flow.

4. *sous le plus pur vocable*. Cf. Mallarmé: 'Donner un sens plus pur aux mots de la tribu' ('Tombeau pour Edgar Poe'), but see note to IV, 6.
un grand Ave *de grâce*. Cf. II, 2 & 4.
tant d'azyme. The word 'azyme' figures in *Anabase*, x, and in his marginal comment on the typescript of Eliot's translation, Perse wrote: 'Il y a là, par transposition, une idée de trans-substantiation, comme dans l'aspect matériel de l'hostie.' Here the taste of the unleavened host has priority over its visual aspect as the sense being transcended.

5. *nous tissera linge plus frais*. Cf. I, I. This cooler raiment replaces the 'cilice du sel' ('Exil', IV, 15) and soothes 'la brûlure des vivants'.
l'hièble du songe. Cf. II, 2: 'un songe de mélèze'.
ta fraîche haleine de mensonge. Cf. note to III, 6.
les grands lés du songe. Cf. I, I.
fongible. The legal term applies both to the snow, 'fungible' into water, and to the mutable world governed by 'usure' against which are posited the permanent values of 'l'être' and, by implication, of 'le devenir'.

6. Cf. Mallarmé: 'le vide papier que la blancheur défend' ('Brise marine') and 'Exil', IV, 21. This and other apparent echoes of Mallarmé (see IV, 3 & 4) might suggest that a similar aesthetics lies behind the two poets' work. Nothing could be further from the truth: all Mallarmé's poetry strives for *fixity*, for the perfect crystallisation of thought in language which is voluntarily *hermetic*. Perse's work is a *dynamic* exploration of the unknown (and the known) expressed with the greatest possible concreteness and clarity. He is much more akin to the open-ended power of the Rimbaud of *Illuminations* than to the controlled obscurity of Mallarmé. Perse sees it as the poet's duty to explore the obscure but to express his findings with the utmost clarity and precision. His is not a poetics of wilful obfuscation. This is not to say that Perse does not appreciate and admire Mallarmé's intellectual power and probity.

'POEME A L'ETRANGERE'

Epigraph: The Alien Registration Act (1940) was the federal law whereby foreigners were required to register at the Aliens' Bureau.

I

2. *des Castilles*. The Spanish origins of the 'Etrangère' are clearly stated.

3. *la maison de bois qui bouge . . . sur ses ancres*. In the context of so much submarine imagery, it is reasonable to take this as an image of a wooden house in the Potomac valley (see Knodel, p. 71). In a letter to Ivan Goll of 10 March 1942, Perse blames his delay in writing to the 'accablement de ces migraines arthritiques que me vaut le climat de Washington, aquarium vraiment trop mal réglé pour un ludion d'Europe'.

à fond d'abîme = 'au fond de l'abîme'. It is an idiosyncrasy with Perse to change a dative possessive phrase to an adverbial one.

mûrit un fruit de lampes à midi. The lights are left burning all day. Cf. I, 11: II, 3: III, 1 & 13.

6. *les ronds-points d'Observatoires*. The Naval Observatory Circle off Massachusetts Avenue. The tram (streetcar) is imagined departing for Atlantis, and so the greenery on the roundabout is seen as sargasso sea-weed.

7. All recognisable districts or features of Washington D.C. The 'migrations d'alevins' suggest, in the underwater imagery of the canto, seething crowds of people, an image appropriate to the 'quartiers de Nègres et d'Asiates'.

8. *hippocampes*. Even the horses of the Federal Cavalry of the American Civil War, remembered in equestrian statues, suffer a sea-change.

9. *chantant l'hier, chantant l'ailleurs*. The unusual use of the demonstrative underlines the metagrammatism.

11. *Rue Gît-le-cœur*. A little street running down to the Seine parallel to the Boulevard St-Michel in Paris VIe, a centre of musical and other activity. Aragon (*SIC*, 31, October 1918) mentions it in the following terms: 'Rue Gît-le-cœur, tu te promènes: n'oublie pas les dessins sur les murs, cœurs empennés, cœurs en peine'.

'l'Alienne': formed on the basis of the English word. Her mistake consists in reading emotional attachments into the street name by considering the meaning of the words whereas the poet is using it simply as a musical refrain evocative of exile. She takes a 'comptine' literally.

II

2. *ô sabre de Strogoff à hauteur de nos cils*. One of Perse's rare direct literary allusions. In Jules Verne's classic thriller *Michel Strogoff*, the tsar's emissary is subjected to a particularly vicious form of torture before the eyes of his mother who has herself suffered torture at the barbarians' hands (Part II, Chap. 5). Strogoff is 'aveuglé suivant la coutume tartare,

avec une lame ardente, passée devant les yeux'. It is not until the final chapter that we learn the truth of this crucial incident. At the risk of spoiling the suspense, I must reveal that because of his deep love for his mother, 'des larmes, que sa fierté essayait en vain de retenir, s'étaient amassées sous ses paupières et, en se volatilisant sur la cornée, lui avait sauvé la vue'. Perse's love for his mother is fully expressed in 'Neiges': the image here underlines the pain involved in constant consideration of the world's violence.

Perse's request to Ivan Goll (in a letter dated 8 March 1943) was never carried out: 'je vous serais obligé de rétablir, sur mon texte, un mot que j'avais rayé pour une question de métrique, mais que je suis obligé de maintenir pour l'interprétation: le mot: "MICHEL" avant Strogoff (L'association, purement visuelle, et bien inactuelle, procédait d'une illustration de Jules Verne)'.

3. *ces trop longs cigares.* Cf. III, 12, where a reference is made to an empty panatella box.

9. *un oiseau . . . vêtu de très beau rouge comme Prince d'Eglise.* An amusing but entirely accurate way to designate the cardinal bird; cf. note to 'Neiges', III, 6.

l'écureuil. Perse connects squirrels with his own state of exile in a letter to Mrs Biddle: 'n'ai-je pas aujourd'hui le même statut que mes amis les écureuils du Central Park et les mouettes de l'"East River", pour qui mon budget d'exilé comportera toujours assez de "pea-nuts" et de "crackers"? Quant à l'exil lui-même, n'est-il pas partout en ce monde, à commencer par le cœur d'une femme? Je le trouve, en tout cas, dans l'œil du petit noir qui me cire les chaussures, et, plus encore, dans l'œil du cheval de police qui me refuse chaque nuit, avec la même douceur, mon morceau de sucre sur la voie publique' (Pléiade, p. 900).

l'enfant-aux-journaux first appeared in English as 'le paper-boy' in the early editions.

10. Louis-Marcel Raymond records the annual nesting of eagles on a Montreal skyscraper ('Humanité de Saint-John Perse', *Honneur*, p. 120). Knodel states that eagles also appeared over Washington (p. 74). This could be a reference to a 'fait divers' recorded in the Pléiade volume (pp. 945, 1257–8), when a pair of 'buzzards' or vultures left circumstantial evidence of their visits on the dome of the Library of Congress, to the consternation of the staff and the amusement of the poet.

12. *cet oiseau . . . d'allure peu catholique.* The 'uncatholic' starling is wittily contrasted with the cardinal bird (II, 9). There is irony in the fact that starlings were introduced from the Old World only in the late-nineteenth century and yet seem particularly 'foreign' to the Etrangère.

13. *les cloches en exil.* Cf. II, 7.

III

1. *Dieux proches ... faces ... closes.* Pierre van Rutten ('Le Langage poétique de Saint-John Perse', Ph.D. thesis, Ottawa 1969, pp. 237–8) suggests a cross-fertilisation of French and English in this evocation, 'proche' (Fr.) meaning 'close' (Eng.). Other English words in the poem ('Starling', 'lawns', 'l'Alienne' echoing the English epigraph, 'paper-boy' in the first editions) and similar occurrences elsewhere in Perse's work (cf. 'sans chiffres ni figures', *Amers*, Chœur, 4) seem to support the suggestion.
lampes à midi, ancres. Cf. I, 3.

3. *le troisième an.* Knodel deduces that the Castilian lady came to Washington in 1939, the last year of the Spanish Civil War. One recalls too that in July 1942, the year of the composition of 'Poème à l'Etrangère', Leger wrote his text 'An III de l'exil' for the French exiled in America (Pléiade, pp. 615–6).
au cœur des althæas. Cf. II, 6.
aux seins des filles d'Eloa. The legend of Eloa is well known through a number of nineteenth-century French poets (e.g. Vigny's 'Eloa' or Lamartine's 'La Chute d'un ange'). Perse's imagination is caught by a subject which for centuries has prompted learned debate: the nature of an angel's 'flesh'. Here he goes further and imagines a colour, widely variable, I am assured, even in the female of the human species, for the 'aréole des seins' of the offspring of Eloa's irregular coupling.
à votre porte close. Note the contrasted attitudes of Etrangère and poet ('portes ouvertes', 'Exil', I, 1), the former wilfully closing her eyes to the marvels around her.

4. *Sibylles.* Cf. III, 17, 'Exil', IV, 4 and 'Pluies', I, 6.

7. *éclat du verre.* The reflection of windows in the summer sun; but cf. 'éclat de verre'.

9. *entre vos hautes malles inécloses.* The sense of insecurity and transience is stressed. Note the insistent references to Europe.
la Vierge du Toril. The realism of Spanish idols is well known, and a bleeding Virgin is appropriate for presiding over the pen where the bull is held before being released into the ring (Sp. 'toril').

10. *Votre Dame des Angoisses.* Perse points his rejection of the Etrangère's belief in 'Our Lady of Sorrows' by changing the possessive adjective. The Virgin is traditionally represented in this guise with her breast pierced by seven swords, emblematic of her seven sorrows.

11. *l'astre de bronze aux grilles des autels.* This completes Perse's evocation of the baroque theatricality manifested by Spanish Catholicism. The tradition of riding on horseback up to the altar rails existed among the ruling classes in Spain and its colonies.

les hautes lances de Bréda. A reference to the Spanish Netherlands and specifically to Velasquez's painting of the surrender of Breda in which lances form a positive palissade behind the Spanish victors.

12. Cf. II, 3.

14. *à perte d'hommes*. Cf. 'à perte de vue': Perse is fond of rejuvenating fixed forms of language in this way.

15. *ce haut quartier de Fondation d'aveugles, de Réservoirs . . .* 'The poet's route may be almost exactly retraced by anyone strolling through the northwest sections of Washington, D.C., with the text of the poem in hand. Across from Dumbarton Oaks [where some friends of Perse's lived before giving their home to the University of Harvard: see Pléiade, pp. 1254–5, note to p. 934] is the School for the Blind, and a little further east are the gullies where cemeteries are enclosed by steel-rod fences, and nearby are a few of the finest old mansions in Washington' (Knodel, p. 188, n. 14). In a letter to MacLeish, Perse wrote: 'ce poème, malgré mon horreur de toute poésie directe ou "personnelle", est malgré moi, dans sa transposition, tout imprégné de ce Georgetown où je vis non loin de vous' (Pléiade, p. 941).

17. *abeilles de phosphore*. The famous Washington fireflies (cf. III, 4), but there may also be a reference to 'l'étrange cachet qui fut jadis celui de ma famille paternelle: avec sa couronne aux huit abeilles dont la deuxième, hors de rang, veut figurer l'envol du cadet de famille vers les Isles-du-Vent' (Pléiade, p. 828).

mon peuple de Sibylles. Cf. III, 4, where the 'Sibylles' are equated with 'lucioles'.

comme en un fond de mer. Note how the underwater imagery continues.

18. *ma chienne d'Europe*. It is of no significance, *pace* various critics, whether this is a factual reminiscence or not.

19. *l'Ange à Tobie*. The familiar story of Tobias in the Apocrypha, with its overtones of exile, revelation, love and praise, involves the Angel's support and intervention. The tale includes curing Tobit's blindness by removing 'la taie sur l'œil' (cf. 'Pluies', VII), but more important for the immediate context is its inclusion of a faithful dog whose colour, however, is not stated. Of various paintings depicting Tobias and the Angel with a *white* dog (cf. III, 18), such as that by Filippino Lippi, the one by Poussin seems best to evoke the sense of exile, the figures being dwarfed by a mass of landscape and greenery rather as the Etrangère's house is inundated by the lushness of the Potomac valley.

BIBLIOGRAPHY

of works to which reference is made

Aragon, 'Critique synthétique' of Apollinaire's *Calligrammes*, *SIC*, 31, October 1918.

Gaston Bachelard, *L'Eau et les rêves*, Corti, 1942.

—, *La Poétique de l'espace*, Presses Universitaires de France, 1957.

Roger Caillois, *Poétique de St.-John Perse*, Gallimard, 1953.

Elizabeth R. Cameron, 'Alexis Saint-Léger Léger' in *The Diplomats, 1919–1939*, Princeton University Press, 1953.

Katherine Garrison Chapin, 'Poet of Wide Horizons', *The Quarterly Journal of the Library of Congress*, XXVII, 2, April 1970, 105–8.

Paul Claudel, *Œuvres en prose*, Gallimard, Bibliothèque de la Pléiade, 1965.

—, *Œuvres poétiques*, Gallimard, Bibliothèque de la Pléiade, 1962.

Charles Dolamore, 'The Love and Aggression of Saint-John Perse's "Pluies"', *Forum for Modern Language Studies*, VII, 3, July 1971, 211–20.

Gilbert Durand, 'Psychanalyse de la neige', *Mercure de France*, CCCXVIII, August 1953, 615–39.

J. G. Frazer, *The Golden Bough*, III: *Taboo and the Perils of the Soul*, Macmillan, 3rd edn, 1911.

Albert Henry, 'Storia e critica interna', *Strumenti critici*, II, 5, February 1968, 80–6.

Arthur J. Knodel, *Saint-John Perse: A Study of his Poetry*, Edinburgh University Press, 1966.

—, 'The Imagery of Saint-John Perse's "Neiges"', *PMLA*, LXX, 1, March 1955, 5–18; also in *Honneur*, pp. 447–60, tr. under title 'Les Images dans "Neiges"'.

Roger Little, *Saint-John Perse*, Athlone Press, 1973.

—, 'Language as Imagery in Saint-John Perse', *Forum for Modern Language Studies*, VI, 2, April 1970, 127–39.

Stéphane Mallarmé, *Œuvres complètes*, Gallimard, Bibliothèque de la Pléiade, 1956.

Charlton Ogburn, 'Comment fut écrit "Pluies"' in *Honneur*, pp. 273–9.

Michel Otten, 'Commentaire de "Exil" de Saint-John Perse', unpubl. seminar, Université de Louvain, 1959–60.

Monique Parent, *Saint-John Perse et quelques devanciers: Etudes sur le poème en prose*, Klincksieck, 1960.

Jean Paulhan and Pierre Oster (eds.), *Honneur à Saint-John Perse*, Gallimard, 1965.

Louis-Marcel Raymond, 'Humanité de Saint-John Perse' in *Honneur*, pp. 110–21.

Pierre van Rutten, 'Le Langage poétique de Saint-John Perse', Ph.D. thesis, University of Ottawa, 1969.

Maurice Saillet, *Saint-John Perse, poète de gloire*, Mercure de France, 1952.

Saint-John Perse, *Œuvres complètes*, Gallimard, Bibliothèque de la Pléiade, 1972.

Jean Schlumberger, 'Rencontres', *NRF*, xv, 176, August 1967, 268–78; also in *Rencontres*, Gallimard, 1968, pp. 24–9.

Michel Soulié, *La Vie politique d'Edouard Herriot*, Colin, 1962.

Simon Watson Taylor and Edward Lucie-Smith (eds.), *French Poetry Today*, Rapp & Whiting/Deutsch, 1971.

G. C. Vaillant, *The Aztecs of Mexico*, Penguin, 1950.

For a select bibliography on Saint-John Perse, see the monograph which is a companion volume to the present edition. Further references may be found in R. Little, *Saint-John Perse: A Bibliography for Students of his Poetry*, Grant & Cutler, Research Bibliographies and Checklists, No. 1, 1971.